Exploring History in and around
DERBYSHIRE

Exploring History in and around
DERBYSHIRE

Richard Stone

breedon **books**
PUBLISHING

First published in Great Britain in 2009 by
The Breedon Books Publishing Company Limited
Breedon House, 3 The Parker Centre,
Derby, DE21 4SZ.

A catalogue record for this book is available from the British Library.

ISBN 978-1-85983-705-4

Printed and bound by TJ International, Padstow, Cornwall.

CONTENTS

For Olivia

Prologue

CRYPTIC TALE

Waxing lyrical about Saxon crypts.

'I was working in the lab late one night, when my eyes beheld an eerie sight.' If you are singing along to *The Monster Mash* by Bobby 'Boris' Pickett and the Crypt Kickers you are giving your age away. It is easy to understand why we associate crypts with the macabre. They tend to be cramped, dark, secretive places tucked away underground. And most were intended for use primarily as burial vaults. On the plus side – oh yes there is one – early crypts offer an unparalleled insight into what we tend to call, with more than a hint of rose-tinted disapproval, the 'Dark Ages'. Half a dozen pre-conquest gems contain some of the best-preserved examples of that rare commodity, Anglo-Saxon architecture.

England before the Normans was for the most part a land of wooden buildings. Even its royal 'palaces' were large timber halls, constructed using carpentry techniques that grew out of boat-building traditions. Consequently, practically nothing remains of any secular building from the period, and while many churches have Saxon features much is fragmentary. For architectural completeness the early crypts that have survived against the odds are hard to match. In the seventh century, St Wilfrid organised a team of stonemasons, glaziers and plasterers from France and Italy to build a church at Ripon in Yorkshire. Today, the tiny crypt is all that remains of his original basilica.

Christchurch Priory, Hampshire, is best known for its wonderful Norman architecture, but buried beneath the transepts and quire lie three crypts of Saxon date. One of these, below the north transept, can be visited and has windows opening onto the churchyard at ground level.

All Saints' Church at Wing in Buckinghamshire, one of the most complete Saxon churches in England, has an unusual polygonal apse. The crypt beneath is a similar shape and may date back to the late-seventh century. Records show the church at Wing housed the relics of an un-named saint until the 10th century, when the remains were transferred to Winchester.

Two sets of steps, one from the north aisle of the nave and another connecting to the south aisle, show where attendant priests once entered and where pilgrims progressed around a central shrine. Recesses in the walls would have been used for important burials.

All Saints' Church, Wing.

St Wystan's Church, Repton.

Visitor access to the crypt at Wing today is via a barrel-vaulted window located on the outside of the apse.

Pilgrims visiting All Saints' Church at Brixworth, Northamptonshire, were led down a flight of steps from a doorway inside the chancel along a tunnelled walkway or ambulatory circling beneath the apse. During restoration the entrance was blocked off but the ambulatory, now roofless, can still be seen outside the eastern end of the church.

St Wystan's Church in Repton, Derbyshire, possesses arguably the most beautiful of Saxon crypts. Here, a simple underground chamber, lined with massive slabs of stone almost a

metre thick, was constructed in the eighth century as a mausoleum for the Mercian royal family. It may have originally been built to receive the body of King Aethelbald, killed by his rebellious kinsman Beornred in 757 following defeat by a West Saxon army at Seckington. A vaulted ceiling was added in 840 to receive the body of King Wiglaf.

Nine years later, Wiglaf's grandson, Wystan, was murdered. Following reports of miracles, the young man became venerated as a martyr and was soon elevated to sainthood to public acclaim (see page 38). As Wystan's cult grew, large numbers of people clamoured to visit his remains and Repton became a place of pilgrimage. A doorway was cut through from the north transept of the nave, with steps leading down to the crypt. Entering today, the top steps are recent additions but it is evident that the shuffling of countless Saxon feet has worn away the lower ones. The square chamber is small, barely five metres across, with a flagstone floor and recesses cut into each of the sides. The semicircular arches of the vaulted roof spring from square pilasters set against walls of smooth, accurately carved masonry. Four round columns, each sculpted from a single block of stone, are decorated with a thin spiral band, like coiled woodbine threading around a tree trunk.

Incredibly, the crypt at Repton was only rediscovered by accident in 1779. Workmen were digging a grave in the chancel floor when one of them fell through. There are similar stories elsewhere. The seventh-century crypt that once contained the relics of St Andrew was uncovered at Hexham Abbey, Northumberland, in 1725 after being lost for centuries. A Saxon crypt at St Giles in Sidbury, Devon, only came to light in 1898. Are there others awaiting rediscovery? I feel sure the answer must be 'Yes', but the constant use and rebuilding that takes place on sites with a long history as consecrated ground disguises the evidence. Another problem is that crypts are invariably located at the east end of the church, below the high altar and chancel. Digging up the most sacred area of ancient churches on an archaeological off chance is not likely to win much support, which makes the few early crypts we do have even more important.

If you have the opportunity to visit one of these rare and special places, and in some cases prior arrangements may be necessary to ensure access, do go and explore. Despite what the Crypt Kickers might suggest, no 'monster from the slab' will begin 'to rise' and any 'surprise' is likely to be in the fascinating history on display. After all, 'it caught on in a flash'.

1

A WATERY RAVE

Exploring a precious resource.

Three weeks without food, three days without water. That is the maximum survival time experts allow a fit, healthy person, and I do not propose putting it to the test. Water is essential to life. Along with air, earth and fire, it is one of the four vital elements venerated in classical antiquity and invested with religious significance from time immemorial. No wonder water has become such an integral part of our culture and customs. Derbyshire's unique well dressing celebrations may contain echoes of ancient sacred rituals.

Natural springs were depended upon for drinking water until the 16th century. Miraculous healing cures were claimed for holy wells. From pre-historic times gifts were tossed into wells in search of divine insight or to propitiate the spirits it was believed dwelt within. Sites with pagan associations were frequently re-dedicated as Christianity was adopted. The names of Annis, the three-headed goddess whose cult thrived in the Iron Age, and Anu, Earth goddess of the Celts, may have translated into St Ann, a possible explanation for the commonness of this name in association with springs, most famously St Ann's Well at Buxton.

The popularity of Buxton's waters is nothing new. Remains of Roman baths were discovered in 1709 when the town's famous Crescent was being built. A spring in the Nook at Stoney Middleton is known as the Roman Bath but is probably a Georgian feature.

St Ann's Well, Buxton.

During the 18th and 19th centuries the supposed health-giving properties of mineral-rich thermal springs began to be exploited at spas. 'Taking the waters' became fashionable. At 68 degrees Fahrenheit, the waters at Matlock were decidedly chilly compared to those at Buxton, bubbling to the surface at a constant 82 degrees, but Smedley's Hydro (now serving as Derbyshire County Council's offices) still prospered. Thermal springs at Bakewell once fed a bathhouse built by the Duke of Rutland. At Kedleston, the Curzon family attempted to cash in on the spa boom by using the village well at Quarndon in tandem with a thermal spring on the estate.

Unfortunately, just as the enterprise was launched a geological hiccup halted the flow of water and doomed the venture to failure. Quarndon's legacy is an impressive gothic frontage for the village 'drip' and a golf course featuring a 'Bath House'.

Jack pumps with handles delivering 'a yard of pump water' replaced the bucket and windlass at village wells from around 1800. A covered well had the added advantage of protecting precious drinking water from being contaminated. A common nickname was the 'cow with the iron tail', a reference to the supposed practice of diluting milk undertaken by unscrupulous dairymen. The village pump was gossip central, where people met and exchanged daily chit-chat.

The village well, Quarndon.

An example of a Jack pump at Ellastone and (inset) Alkmonton.

The Twelve Apostles, Ible.

Roman villas enjoyed sophisticated plumbing, but the technology vanished with the legions and it was not until the Middle Ages that piped water became available once more for those with sufficient money to invest.

Troughs served the needs of people and livestock in many villages. A series of stone basins by the roadside at Ible are known locally as the 'Twelve Apostles'.

At Eyam an ingenious series of spring-fed troughs represent one of the earliest integrated public water systems. One pair of troughs accessed separate sources to supply hard water for drinking and soft water for washing clothes.

The spring-fed water troughs, Eyam.

WATER LANE TROUGHS

The set of two troughs dating from 1588 were used for drinking water. Close by is another trough which supplied soft water. The wives would meet here on washday to wash their clothes and then spread them on the adjoining parish land to dry.

Bolsover.

A well-house in the courtyard at Bolsover Castle was fed by lead piping from conduit houses built along a line of springs on a nearby hillside.

Youlgreave's 'Fountain', a gritstone conduit head storing water piped from a spring across the valley, was built to supply the village in 1829.

Youlgreave 'Fountain'.

Victorian England's increased understanding and concern for public health began the gradual process of ensuring a clean, piped water supply was made available to all. Fear of cholera spurred activity. Since arriving in England in the early 1830s, epidemics of this highly infectious and frequently fatal bacterial disease became regular occurrences. Contaminated water supplies and lack of sanitation were the chief causes. Often progress towards a healthy water system depended upon local benefactors rather than the authorities. At Ashbourne, the champion was Captain Holland of Ashbourne Hall. A solitary street pump, rescued from the Market Place and now re-sited in Belle View Road, is a testament to his efforts in the 1890s.

At Ticknall, it was local squires the Harpur-Crewes who footed the bill for installing the lion-headed cast-iron water pumps that still dot the village streets today.

Revd Hervey Wilmot Sitwell was the benefactor at Horsley, providing the first piped water supply in 1864. The three outlets in the village were called Sophia, after his wife; and Rosamund and Blanche after two great-nieces born that year.

South Staffordshire Water Works, formed in 1853, was among the earliest private water companies. Based in Walsall, the first town to receive a piped water supply from the company was

A cast-iron water pump, Ticknall.

The Horsley Sitwell 'fountains'. Sophia (left), Rosamund (middle) and Blanche (right).

Wednesbury. An agreement was reached with the town commissioners of Burton upon Trent for the company to replace household wells with a properly filtered, piped supply in 1864. Conveniently, a new bridge across the River Trent was nearing completion, providing an ideal platform to carry water pipes over the river.

For a town riddled with wells and boreholes, between them supplying millions of gallons daily for Burton's brewing industry, it is perhaps a little perverse that the first piped water came from Lichfield. Then, in 1891, a 180ft well was sunk at Fradley (on a site close to the Coventry Canal beside a track known as Ironstone Lane) and a pumping station was built to house two horizontal compound tandem Davey-type engines. One engine was always working and the second kept 'belt and braces' style in reserve for emergencies.

From Fradley, water was pumped to a reservoir, constructed by Henry Lovatt of Wolverhampton, on the summit of the Outwoods Hills, on the north-west outskirts of the town. Mains pressure, necessary to avoid contamination as well as to ensure a steady supply, was maintained by gravity. Although on a larger scale it works on exactly the same principle as a header tank in a domestic loft.

The altitude of the Outwoods reservoir, 319ft above sea level, was sufficient to keep mains pressure high for most of the town. The higher residential areas of Winshill, and to a lesser extent Stapenhill (both in Derbyshire until 1874), were a problem. Many residents had to walk downhill to find a working street pump. By the turn of the 20th century, higher standards were expected.

Fradley pumping station.

In 1904, South Staffordshire Water Company drew up plans for a water tower on Waterloo Mount, the highest part of Burton marking the ancient boundary between Stapenhill and Winshill. It had been named in a burst of patriotic enthusiasm after the defeat of Napoleon in 1815. Lord of the Manor at Burton, Henry Paget, 1st Marquis of Anglesey, had been in charge of the cavalry and second in command to the Duke of Wellington at the Battle of Waterloo.

Constructed, as was Fradley pumping station, by local builders Thomas Lowe, the 80ft-high tower is a solidly extravagant tour de force of brickwork, its outward appearance resembling the keep of a great mediaeval castle. Visible up to 25 miles away, the tower became an instant landmark. Generations of locals returning from their travels have looked for the distinctive silhouette on the skyline and on spotting it, gratefully murmured: 'Nearly home'.

The storage tank at the top of tower is 496ft above sea level and fitted with electrically driven centrifugal pumps, linked to a float switch, that cut in automatically to ensure a minimum depth of 7ft of water at all times. With the addition of small pumping stations at strategic high points, the tower was high enough to solve all the town's water supply

The Water Tower on Waterloo Mount, Burton upon Trent.

An example of a mere, near Larkstone Wood, Wetton.

problems when it was linked into the system operationally in 1907. More recently, the tower has acquired a new purpose carrying communication masts.

In the limestone uplands of the White Peak rainwater drains quickly through the porous bedrock. Here the answer was the construction of artificial meres, originally made waterproof by puddling clay with straw and later using concrete. Building meres and choosing the best sites to collect precious rainfall was a specialist job carried out by small teams of men who travelled from farm to farm. Their work is still evident today in the corners of fields throughout the White Peak.

It was the 1940s before piped water reached many rural areas. Redundant village wells were neglected. Many disappeared, but in recent years some, for example the well on Brackenfield's expansive village green, have been restored.

No doubt about it, water is wonderful stuff, though these days we may be tempted to take our supply a little too much for granted.

The restored well at Brackenfield.

2

FULL FONT-AL

Fascinating fonts.

It is a familiar scene. Proud parents with family and friends gathered around. All eyes on the baby cradled in the vicar's arms. Few parish churches are without a font, usually just inside the main entrance, symbolising spiritual as well as physical access. Back in the 1230s, Archbishop of Canterbury, Edmund Rich ordered: 'There shall be a font of stone or other competent material in every church'. Stone is generally the material of choice but 'other competent material' opens up possibilities.

At All Saints' Church, Ashover, a Norman font dating from the mid-12th century is a rare example of a stone basin encased entirely in lead. The metal has been beautifully worked to show apostle figures within an arcade encircling the bowl. Given Derbyshire's long tradition of lead mining you would expect there to be others like it. In fact, it is the only lead font in the county as far as I know and is lucky to have survived at all. During

The lead casing of the font at All Saints' Church, Ashover.

the English Civil War lead was scavenged from any available source to be melted down for musket shot. Rector Immanuel Bourne had the foresight to bury Ashover's font in his garden at Eastwood Hall. Disgruntled Parliamentary forces paid him back by devastating the building, though not without difficulty, as Bourne's clerk, Wheatcroft, recorded in verse:

> The Roundheads came down to Eastwood Hall,
> And they tried it with mattocks and they tried it with ball,
> And they tore up the leadwork and splintered the wood,
> But as firmly as ever the battlements stood,
> Till a barrel of gunpowder at last did the thing,
> And then they sang psalms for the fall of the King.

In addition to blowing up the hall, All Saints' Church was vandalised by Parliamentarian soldiers and the parish registers, in Latin and therefore considered 'Popish', were destroyed. By all accounts, the Revd Bourne was something of a self-publicist but if he is to be believed, his action kept the remarkable bowl safe. Before moving on, it is said the Roundhead commander preached a sermon, in response to which Bourne scoffed, 'Lord what stuff and nonsense he did talk, and if he could have murdered the King as easily as he did the King's English, the war long since would have been over'.

Many parish churches had fonts long before Archbishop

Eastwood Hall.

The font at St Leonard's, Thorpe.

The ancient font at St Chad's, Church Wilne, with the carving of a dragon just visible.

Rich's edict. There are Saxon fonts at St Michael's, Earl Sterndale; Church of the Holy Cross, Morton; St Lawrence's, Eyam; and St Leonard's, Thorpe. The font of St Peter's, Parwich, has a Norman bowl with a later stem.

Almost certainly the oldest font in Derbyshire is at St Chad's, Church Wilne. Within this secluded church, moored on the flood plain between the rivers Derwent and Trent, is a simple tub that may date from the time when Chad himself, appointed Bishop of Lichfield in 669, was preaching the gospel with missionary zeal across the Anglian kingdom of Mercia. Though age-worn and fire damaged, an intricate carving of a dragon surrounded by birds and an interlace pattern remains visible.

Fonts mirror the age in which they were made. Naïve carvings on a Saxon font just across the county boundary in Holy Cross Church, Ilam, show scenes from the life of St Bertram whose shrine is housed within the church. St Michael and St Mary, Melbourne,

The font at Ilam, showing scenes from the life of St Bertram.

has a model of unaffected early 13th-century simplicity. The font at St Oswald's, Ashbourne, with its pointed moulding and restrained leaf motifs, is a consummate example of 13th-century Early Gothic. As buildings became more decorated during the 14th and 15th centuries, eight-sided fonts with elaborate tracery became popular, reflecting changing architectural styles.

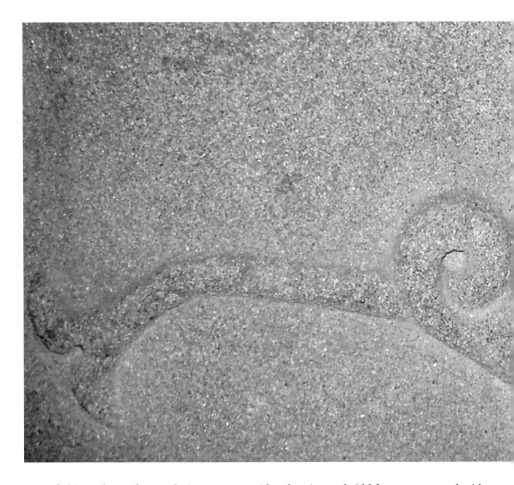

As fashions changed some designs were considered antiquated. Old fonts were tossed aside or put to alternative uses. A 12th-century bowl from St Michael and All Angels, Taddington, was used for washing glasses in the Star Inn until it was rescued in 1939. Decorators once used the font of St John the Baptist, Tideswell, as the parish paint pot. In the years following the Reformation, many fonts were considered to have 'inappropriate' imagery by those with strict Puritan views and were destroyed. An interesting 15th-century octagonal font at St John the Baptist Church, Chelmorton, is decorated with mysterious signs.

Among the more individual stylistic flourishes, a font at All Saints' Church, Youlgreave, has an extra stoup, possibly intended for holy oil. Beneath the projection, curving around the base of the bowl, is the sculpted figure of a salamander. In ancient mythology, this legendary beast was reputed to be able to survive fire and so came to symbolise purification and virtue. Originally the font belonged to neighbouring Elton. When All Saints' Church there was renovated it was replaced. After a number of years as a garden

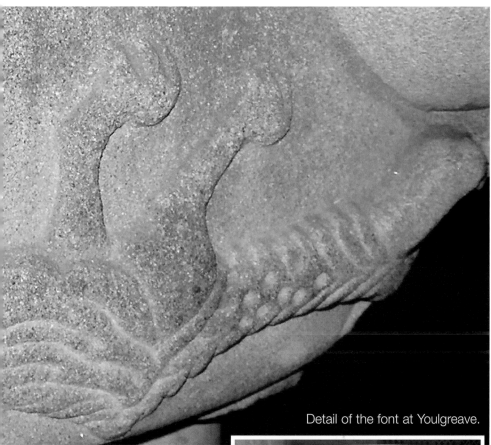

Detail of the font at Youlgreave.

feature it was spotted and snapped up by an enterprising vicar of Youlgreave. Elton now has a replica.

Youlgreave's font is not the only one in Derbyshire with a salamander motif. A font at Holy Trinity, Ashford-in-the-Water, is similarly decorated and also spent some time as a garden ornament.

What to do with baptismal water after use was once a problem. Since it had been blessed, simply throwing it away was considered impious. Left in the font it soon became unhygienic and a danger to health. Archbishop Rich's injunction included instructions that the water '…shall not be kept above seven days in the font'. He also decreed that fonts should be covered because consecrated water was a target for groups dabbling in dark arts. Simple wooden lids were introduced in many churches that could be secured by an iron bar, padlocked between iron staples. A 12th-century font in the chapel at Haddon Hall that once served the parishioners of the now deserted mediaeval village of Nether Haddon, displays the scars of damage caused by fastenings hammered into the stone rim. More elaborate heavy covers began to be introduced in the late 17th century. Some were so weighty that block and pulley tackle was needed to raise them. These days baptismal water is blessed on the day it is required.

Baptism has always been the rite of entrance to the Christian Church. Early converts were baptised in rivers. Since then, fonts in parish churches have welcomed countless generations. Until recent times, where a sprinkle is deemed sufficient, bowls were large enough to allow for the partial immersion of infants. In the mediaeval period it was mainly adults who were baptised. Nowadays, christening of infants is the normal practice. Communion has become the principal sacrament and the font has been relegated to something of a ritual prop, often barely noticed unless a baptism is taking place. But it is not just the old, rare, unusual, or those with a chequered history that are of interest. Collectively and individually all of our fonts have their own fascinating story to tell.

3

SAINTS ALIVE

A glimpse behind the haloes of those strange sounding saints to whom some of our local churches are dedicated.

In the 10th century, the Church took control of decisions about who became a saint. By that time some obscure, colourful and deserving characters had already entered the canon, promoted through the rather more democratic process of public acclamation.

The parish church of Burton upon Trent is dedicated to the town's patron saint, the obscure Modwen. Rather better known is Chad, who features at Lichfield and elsewhere, but then we have Werburgh (Derby, Blackwell, Spondon, Kingsley, Hanbury); Wystan (Repton, Bretby); Cuthbert (Doveridge); Hardulph (Breedon on the Hill); not to mention Bertram (Ilam); Editha (Tamworth); and Oswald (Ashbourne) – none of whom are exactly household names. And who was St Bride? Why does a farmhouse near Melbourne bear her name?

St Bride's farmhouse.

Early saints were a robust breed. What we know of their lives is drawn from ambiguous references and sketchy accounts that in most cases were written down by mediaeval chroniclers long after the events described. Myth and legend inevitably interweave with fact.

Faced with the daunting task of spreading the gospel to some 2,000,000 pagans with no mass media, the missionaries despatched to our shores by Pope Gregory in 597 had clear instructions about how to make best use of their limited resources – concentrate on the royals. Win over the leaders and the subjects will follow was the plan. Convince the kings that they are divinely appointed instruments of destiny, chosen by God to lead their people to be saved. As a message it played well. It is hardly surprising that the early history of the English Church is littered with saints and martyrs of noble birth as one by one, the mini-kingdoms that made up Anglo-Saxon England abandoned Woden and Thor in favour of Christianity.

Oswald was of the Northumbrian royal line. When his uncle, Edwin, seized the throne, he was exiled to the monastery on Iona where Aidan was a monk. While there he was baptised in the Christian faith. Aidan went on to found a monastery at Lindisfarne. In possibly the first recorded instance of 'pouring oil on troubled waters', Bede recorded how a flask of oil blessed by Aidan calmed a stormy sea. Penda, Mercia's pagan ruler, who based his court at Repton, despatched both Edwin and Oswald on their way to canonisation. Penda claimed descent from Woden himself and his gods were the heroes of Scandinavian mythology, but his argument with the Northumbrians was political rather than religious. Edwin's death in 632 opened the way for Oswald to return and claim his birthright. Ten years later Oswald made the mistake of tackling Penda in battle and ended up in several pieces. In Saxon England, a violent death rather than piety seems to have been the main requirement for canonisation. Oswald's 'bits' were eventually recovered and reburied (for more on Penda, see chapter 28).

Cuthbert served as abbot of Lindisfarne before retiring to a contemplative life as a hermit on the rather more remote Farne Islands. After his death in 687 his body was taken back to Northumbria. Towards the close of the eighth century, Viking raids forced the monks of Lindisfarne to abandon the abbey. They took St Cuthbert's remains with them for safekeeping and in their haste popped Oswald's skull in the same coffin. A frontal lobe was rediscovered in 1899.

Christianity spread in Derbyshire when Prince Peada of Mercia married Princess Alhflaed of Northumbria. The newlyweds returned to Repton with four priests in tow. One of them, Diuma, became the first bishop of Mercia. Another, Cedd, elder brother of Chad,

The sculpture of St Modwen on the Trent Washlands, Burton upon Trent.

went on to become bishop of the East Angles. All probably began their mission as novice monks at Aidan's monastery on Lindisfarne and all later achieved sainthood.

According to tradition, a seventh-century Irish nun from Dundalk called Modwen, daughter of a chief of Clan Conall, set off with two companions on a pilgrimage to Rome. She stopped off at Burton and founded a religious community beside the River Trent. After her death in Scotland, Modwen's body was returned to Burton where her shrine became a place of pilgrimage. Miraculous cures were attributed to the water from a nearby well. The

veneration of relics and objects was outlawed as superstitious nonsense during the Reformation. An image of St Modwen was removed from the shrine at Burton and taken to London on the express orders of no less a person than Thomas Cromwell, lord chamberlain to Henry VIII. Clearly this confiscated representation of St Modwen was an object of considerable value, possibly of gold or silver. It was never seen again and in all probability was melted down.

Anchor Church, near Foremark.

Today, St Modwen is back beside the river at Burton. This time conceived as a striking modern wind sculpture by John Fortnum, a dominant silhouette on the flat washlands.

One early text tells how Modwen met with a hermit called Hardulche who was living a life of austerity near to Burton in a cell hewn out of a rock face. Anchor Church, by the River Trent near Foremark, fits the description and Hardulche has been identified with Hardulph after whom the Priory Church of St Mary and St Hardulph at Breedon on the Hill is named. However, a 12th-century document contains a reference to an Aerdulfus Rex, a king of the lost dark centuries rather than a hermit, who was laid to rest at Breedon.

Among an exceptional collection of Anglo-Saxon stone carvings at Breedon is a frieze some 12 centuries old depicting three male saints, complete with haloes, who may be buried at Breedon. The trio is assumed to be Cotta, Benna and Fretheric, who sound as though they ought to be members of a Swedish pop group (incidentally, 'Abba' is also old Aramaic for 'Holy Father' or 'bishop' and is the root of our words abbey and abbot). Sadly, only their names and nothing at all of their lives is known. Perhaps in some ways the early saints were the pop stars of their day, powerful performers capable of drawing and holding an audience. If saints were still chosen by public adulation we would surely have St Elvis by now.

Bride was a simple Irish cowgirl baptised, it is said, by St Patrick himself. Among the miracles attributed to her was an ability to turn her bath water into beer or for her cow to produce extra milk if unexpected guests arrived. It is hard to come up with an explanation for a local dedication but in open countryside between Ticknall and Melbourne is St

Anglo-Saxon sculpture depicting three saints, Breedon on the Hill.

St Rufin's Well, Tamworth.

Bride's farm. Is it possible Modwen was inspired by her countrywoman (early references associate Modwen with a cow) and brought stories of her to the local area? Once an outpost of Burton Abbey, the private house and recent barn conversions now on the site are built around what appears to be the nave of an early-mediaeval chapel. Ancient trackways converge at this spot including a bridleway that in former times was the main road from Derby to Oxford, its route passing through Melbourne along what was once Bride Street, now renamed High Street. St Bride's tunic turned up in the 11th century. King Harold's sister Gunnhilda presented it to St Donation's Church in Bruges where, as far as I know, it can still be found.

According to tradition, Prince Wulfad, son of pagan King Wulfhere, was in pursuit of a stag when he chanced upon Chad, the Northumbrian monk recently appointed Bishop of Mercia. Chad was sitting by a spring, near the humble cell he had made home. Chad told Wulfad their meeting was no accident. He had sent the stag to lead the young prince to him so that he could be converted. Wulfad's scoffing was silenced when Chad knelt in prayer and the stag obediently trotted out of the woods and approached the two men. Suitably impressed, Wulfad listened to Chad and was baptised.

Back home, Wulfad told his brother Rufin of the encounter and of his conversion.

St Chad's Well, Lichfield.

When the stag reappeared next day, Rufin followed the animal and like his brother was guided to Chad's cell where he too was baptised. Afterwards the brothers secretly visited Chad for religious instruction. When word of what was happening reached Wulfhere, the king insisted his sons renounce their new faith. A stubborn refusal sent him into a rage and in his anger he killed them.

Guilt-ridden and full of remorse after the event, Wulfhere resolved to meet Chad and seek forgiveness. The stag materialised and led the King to where Chad was celebrating mass. Wulfhere was persuaded to convert and promote Christianity throughout his kingdom. Wulfad and Rufin were buried together at Stone. Pilgrims came to pray at their shrine and many miracles were attributed to the martyred princes' intercession.

St Rufin's Chapel, Burston.

It is a colourful tale and one that has left plenty of reminders which are still around today. Tucked into a corner of Tamworth Castle grounds, in the shadow of Ankerside Shopping Centre, is the site of an ancient well dedicated to St Rufin. A cairn built over the princes' grave by their mother Ermenilda is said to give the town of Stone its name. A one-and-a-half-hectare hillfort on Bury Bank, strategically placed above a crossing of the Trent near Stone and reoccupied in Anglo-Saxon times, may be Wulfherecaster, site of Wulfhere's royal palace. Stone's parish church, dedicated to St Michael and St Wulfad, occupies the site of a convent and an early-mediaeval priory established around Wulfhere's burial place. St Rufin's Chapel in the nearby village of Burston stands on the spot where tradition holds Rufin was slain. The redbrick chapel replaced a much earlier building in 1859. St Chad's Well, the spring that was the scene of so much of the action, and a draw for pilgrims ever since, sits in the churchyard of St Chad's, embraced now by suburban Lichfield.

Is any of the story of St Chad and the stag true? The dates fit. Wulfhere ruled Mercia (and most of southern England for that matter) from 657 until his death in 678. Chad was appointed Bishop of Mercia in 669. But, unfortunately, history does not support much else in the legend. Only one son of Wulfhere and Ermenilda is known about and his name was Coenred. Wulfhere was a Christian king who generously endowed Peterborough Abbey. Chad's appointment as Bishop of Mercia was the result of a direct request from Wulfhere to Theodore, Archbishop of Canterbury. The monks who wrote down the tale (and no doubt, the brothers of Stone Priory 'sexed-up' the original 'dossier' later to add to the prestige of their establishment and attract more pilgrims and their offerings) neatly circumvented the facts by claiming Wulfhere had been Christian but reverted to paganism under the influence of an evil counsellor.

I think it would be wrong to dismiss the whole story as fabrication. Wulfad and Rufin have left too many reminders. Perhaps two real-life brothers were martyred for their faith and the monks invented a royal connection simply to give them a credible pedigree to add to the story's impact. Perhaps we should pardon Wulfhere; and if you want to celebrate, the feast day of Wulfad and Rufin is 24 July.

Mercia's first homegrown saint of any real provenance is Werburgh, Wulfhere's daughter. Werburgh headed up a priory at Hanbury established either by her father or more likely by her uncle, Aethelred, who succeeded Wulfhere as ruler of Mercia. Nothing remains of the priory building today, but a fragment of carved sandstone incorporated into the masonry of the south porch of St Werburgh's Church may have come from an original consecration cross. Kindness to animals was among the virtues attributed to Werburgh. According to one legend, she penned up a flock of wild geese overnight for eating priory crops, releasing them the following morning with a warning not to return. When it was discovered that a convent servant had taken advantage of the situation to help himself to a goose supper, Werburgh ordered the bones to be brought to her and restored the bird to life.

Wystan, another of the Mercian royal line, was the son of King Wimund. He was murdered by his godfather, Brifardus, after suggesting that a proposal of marriage to his mother, the widowed Queen Aelfleda, was motivated solely by desire for power. Reports of miracles followed his untimely end. Rumour spread that a column of light shone for 30 days at the place in Shropshire where the dirty deed was done. The site became known as Wystan's 'stow', a word signifying a holy place. Modern Wistanstow village is a little over one mile north of Craven Arms.

Wystan was buried in the royal mausoleum at Repton in 849. The site soon began to attract pilgrims and this is probably the time when a passage was cut through the one metre-thick stone wall of the crypt. Offerings brought by pilgrims made shrines potentially lucrative businesses and so access would have been important.

Bertram was also a local lad of noble birth. Early sources record that he travelled to Ireland to abduct and marry a princess. By the time their long honeymoon journey back was nearly over, the new bride was close to giving birth. Bertram left her alone in the forest while he went to fetch help. He returned to find both wife and baby attacked and partially devoured by wolves. Heartbroken and guilt ridden at the tragedy, Bertram dedicated his life to the church and became a disciple of Guthlac, a reformed tearaway. Guthlac trained as a monk at Repton Priory where it is claimed he cured headaches by ringing a holy bell (fancy trying that on your next hangover?).

Traditionally, Bertram spent his life preaching the gospel around Ilam, living for a while in a rocky recess at Beeston Tor, a steep, jackdaw-haunted crag beside the River Manifold not far from the village of Wetton. Pilgrims still visit the tomb of St Bertram at the Church of the Holy Cross, Ilam, and leave their prayers for intercession written on cards and scraps of paper.

Another folk tale involving the cave on Beeston Tor tells of Talcen, a Celtic prince, who journeyed to Saxon Mercia early in the ninth century. He came carrying gifts and accompanied by a band of followers to seek the hand of Aethelfleda, 'Lady of the Mercians', widowed daughter of King Alfred. Offended by rejection and fearing loss of face if he returned home, Talcen instead joined forces with Aethelfleda's Danish enemies. In a battle at Derby, the Saxons led by the princess won a convincing victory, but Aethelfleda died soon afterwards at Tamworth. On hearing the news a tormented Talcen turned his back on the world. The account concludes that he went to live with a holy man in a secluded cave where he buried his possessions.

Spurned love and a hidden hoard of valuables are familiar enough themes in myth and legend. Then, in September 1924, amateur archaeologist Revd G.H. Wilson from Manchester, while exploring the fissure on Beeston Tor, still known locally as St Bertram's Cave, turned up a treasure trove of gold rings and silver coins all dating to the ninth century, the period of the legend. The finds are now in the British Museum.

Editha, to whom the parish church at Tamworth is dedicated, has been identified with Eadgyth, sister of King Athelstan and who was briefly married to the Hiberno-Norse King Sihtric as part of a peace treaty. Sihtric abandoned her and resumed hostilities within months of the wedding. However, St Editha is more likely to have been the daughter of King Egbert who founded Polesworth Abbey in 827 and appointed his daughter as the first abbess. After the Norman Conquest, the Marmion Barons of Tamworth Castle evicted the nuns from their land and the church at Polesworth. According to legend the abbey was returned to the sisters in 1139, after St Editha appeared one night to wake Robert Marmion from his sleep, striking him on the

St Bertram's Cave, Beeston Tor.

forehead with her crozier and threatening eternal damnation unless the nuns were reinstated.

During the papacy of John Paul II, more than 500 new saints were created. They included some directly relevant to the modern world such as St Isidore of Seville (560–636), who became the patron saint of internet users. There are lots of dedications to early saints still around. Do keep a look out. You will not find a 'Pip' or a 'Squeak' but you only have to go as far as Egginton, Barrow-on-Trent or Ilkeston to find Wilfrid.

4

BRIDGE OF SIZE

Secluded Coldwall Bridge is the legacy of a once busy cross-county turnpike.

For much of its length, the River Dove marks the boundary between Staffordshire and Derbyshire. A variety of foot and road bridges, ancient and modern, provide crossings. They are often hardly noticed as they serve their intended purpose, but Coldwall Bridge is different.

In 1994, an extension of the Limestone Way opened, picking up a network of quiet footpaths taking walkers from Matlock to Rocester. It crosses the River Dove by Coldwall Bridge. The last thing a casual walker expects to find on this grassy route is a massively buttressed, 18ft-wide stone structure complete with milestone declaring 'Cheadle 11 [miles]' on an iron plate dated 1822. A single, segmental arch spans the Dove linking to a causeway that crosses the valley floor into Staffordshire, ending where rising ground clears the immediate flood plain. From here a track leads by Coldwall Farm to the edge of Blore

Coldwall Bridge and (inset) the milestone.

Olde Star Inn, Oakamoor.

village. The milestone is a clue to why such a solid bridge was built. This was once an important turnpike linking the main Derby to Newcastle-under-Lyme road at Blythe Marsh with coaching routes from Ashbourne to Leek and Buxton.

Turnpikes were introduced widely in the 18th and early-19th century when travel difficulties threatened to constrain the opportunities offered by a new industrial age. The Staffordshire Moorlands had rich reserves of copper and iron but roads were poor. Muddy quagmires in wet weather, baked into rutted switchbacks by summer sun. Maintenance of routeways, technically a responsibility shared between parishes and county authorities, was haphazard and minimal. According to local landowner John Leveson-Gower, a retired admiral, the Bay of Biscay in a storm was preferable to being in a carriage around Dilhorne.

Turnpikes were authorised by private Acts of Parliament and allowed a board of trustees to charge road users a toll. Revenue raised was used for maintenance and repair. The Cheadle Trust was approved in 1762 to take charge of what, though well used, was little more than a cross-county track used by farmers and packhorses. The Cheadle Turnpike Trustees set about making improvements immediately. Contractors were employed to level different sections of the road and lay a surface of broken stone and compacted gravel. The turnpike was built with a camber to aid drainage. At the crown was an 18in layer of hardcore. The specification was increased to a minimum depth of 2ft of stone across the full width of the carriageway approaching the bridge at Oakamoor where the land was prone to flood. At Coldwall, a narrow wooden bridge across the Dove was replaced in stone.

The former tollhouse located at Stanton Dale crossroads.

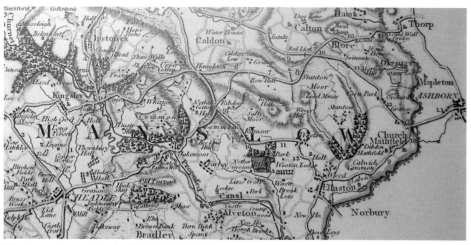

The turnpike route via Coldwall Bridge.

This was not easy country for travellers. Parts of the route rise to over 1,100ft. However, diversions were cut to take the sting out of the two most dangerous inclines. East of Cheadle, an existing route by Highshutt Farm to Oldfurnace and Stoney Dale was bypassed and a new road commissioned. Instructions to T. Burgess, the contractor chosen for the job, were that no part of the route should have a gradient exceeding one in 12. A steep climb out of the Churnet Valley from Oakamoor to Cotton was replaced with a stretch of road laid between limestone walls at Star Bank. The new route sidelined the Olde Star Inn beside the old path forcing the business to relocate.

For the first time, the inhabitants of the Staffordshire Moorlands had ready access to potential markets. A 15-mile journey along the length of the turnpike from Blythe Marsh to Thorpe via Forsbrook, Cheadle, Oakamoor, Cotton, Calton Moor, Bloor and Coldwall Bridge, that previously would have taken all day, could now be completed by a light carriage or on horseback in less than two hours. Good road surfaces and the invention of elliptical springs made travelling a pleasure. People began to take carriage rides for enjoyment as well as out of necessity. New inns opened along the route to provide passing trade with refreshments and comfort stops.

The turnpike brought prosperity to some but of course there was a cost to users. Between Blythe Marsh and Coldwall Bridge, the Cheadle Trust set up no less than nine gates each with a tollhouse. There was a 10th beyond Thorpe, where the road joined the Ashbourne to Buxton road. Charges, displayed on boards at each toll point, varied according to the type and size of vehicle, goods carried or livestock herded. Carriages and wagons were often charged per wheel. Sheep cost less to transport than cattle. Tickets could be bought enabling travellers to cover more than one stage with a single payment. The wealthy employed a running footman to race ahead and pay in advance to avoid being held up at the tollgate.

Business was so brisk on the Cheadle turnpike that Coldwall Bridge became a bottleneck. The new road was designed for two-way traffic. Coldwall Bridge was a single lane just 9ft wide. In the early-19th century to speed the traffic flow, the bridge was widened by a further 9ft on the downstream side. From below, the masonry of the arch clearly shows where the extension took place.

Spiralling maintenance costs and the imminent arrival of the railway presaged the end of an era. Turnpikes began to close. Traffic between Caltonmoor crossroads and Coldwall Bridge lessened and this stretch was freed from toll in 1831. From Caltonmoor to Cheadle, the Trust continued to turn a healthy profit into the 1870s. This was partly because the railway came late to the Staffordshire Moorlands. It was 1849 before the Churnet Valley Line opened and 1892 before a branch line to Cresswell linked Cheadle to the main rail network. Perhaps also it was a reflection of a well-run turnpike and the economic importance of the route in a relatively remote area. The Cheadle Turnpike Trust was one of the last to close. In 1888, responsibility for all road maintenance was transferred to a newly formed county council. In the years that followed some roadside inns, for example the Red Lion at Caltonmoor, and some tollhouses became private residences. Former tollhouses, some substantially rebuilt but sensitively retaining distinctive features, are recognisable from their prominent roadside positions and windows designed to provide a clear view of approaching traffic and to double as paypoints.

The strategic potential of Coldwall Bridge was recognised in the dark days of 1941 when a German invasion was considered a serious threat. To confuse any stray enemy paratrooper, the milestone was temporarily removed. Possibly the solid masonry blocks of this isolated bridge set so incongruously on a footpath would have been puzzle enough.

By the time Coldwall Bridge slipped into retirement the first motorised carriages had appeared. Most of the old turnpike is still in use, resurfaced with asphalt and travelled by modern vehicles. Instead of dipping down by Coldwall Farm to Coldwall Bridge, a new road now takes drivers to Ashbourne across the River Dove at Okeover, two miles south; or to Thorpe via Ilam and St Mary's Bridge to the north. But maybe on nights when the moon rides low, its reflection skimming the waters beneath, an occasional coach still rattles and flies across Coldwall.

5

BLADON FOOL

Nobody likes a show off.

Thumbing your nose at public opinion has always been a risky business. Two hundred years ago the divide between the 'haves' and the 'have nots' was wide. Domestic service was the most common occupation, making the middle classes, collectively, the country's largest employer of labour. Society was organised along rigid class lines. Rank and wealth was accompanied by privilege. But status came with responsibility and expectations about socially acceptable behaviour. England's aristocrats had France as an example of what could happen if things turned nasty. In Paris, the Bastille had been stormed, Doctor Guillotin's helpful suggestions taken up enthusiastically by the mob and the 'Reign of Terror' triggered. Although the mood was very different on this side of the Channel, you would expect some lessons to have been learned about the dangers of conspicuous consumption. Yet this was the time one local man decided on a touch of swank and flashy self-advertisement.

In 1795, Abraham Hoskins, a successful solicitor with a number of business interests, purchased a parcel of land at Newton Solney in south Derbyshire from Sir Henry Every. Hoskins had risen to the position and status of High Bailiff of Burton upon Trent. At 66 years of age he was winding down to enjoy his leisure and set about creating a lifestyle to match his new status as a landowning squire. Up-and-coming designer Francis Bernasconi, known primarily for his elaborate plasterwork, produced plans for an impressive Italianate mansion set in landscaped parkland. No problem so far, Hoskins was simply reaping the rewards of a successful career. Trouble began when a frivolous addition was built half-a-mile south-west of the new park.

Hoskins was a respected pillar of society. His family's status as key players in local society was confirmed when Sarah, Abraham Hoskins's daughter, married Burton brewer Michael Bass. Their son, Michael Thomas Bass, took over the family firm aged 28 in 1827, and with partners Samuel Ratcliff and John Gretton turned it into the greatest brewery in the world.

I suspect Abraham Hoskins junior is the man responsible for the 'added extra'. Then in his late 30s he was an indulged eldest son, very much a man of his age, and in the 18th and

19th centuries there was a fashion for elaborate architectural conceits known collectively as follies (from the French *folie* meaning a delight or favourite place). Rich landowners with plenty of leisure and fat wallets exercised their imaginations on increasingly bizarre designs. Many drew inspiration from their 'Grand Tours' of continental Europe's classic sites, popular jaunts for the well heeled temporarily curtailed by war with France. Practical jokes in stone, brick and mortar including Greek temples, Roman arches, Swiss Bridges, Chinese pagodas and strikingly conceived towers appeared in the grounds of great houses. At Sudbury Hall, Lord Vernon built a fanciful, fortress-like deercote in 1723. His heir followed this some 50 years later with a mediaeval-style tower looking out over the Dove Valley from Tutbury Castle.

Hoskins's folly was Bladon Castle. Built along the prominent summit of Bladon Hill on the Derbyshire bank of the River Trent, to a plan by top architect Sir Jeffrey Wyatville. The 'castle' consisted of a single long wall, pierced by pointed windows and topped with commanding battlements. Like a kite flown on an invisible string from the 'big house', it floated above the ridge, dominating the skyline of Newton Solney and defiantly overlooking Burton upon Trent. From a distance, Bladon Castle had the appearance of the genuine article. Like a modern film set, it was all front. Designed to command attention, possibly to promote Newton Solney as the 'in' place to live and attract investment, the 'castle' certainly caused a stir. An antagonistic local mood is even more understandable seen in the context of the times and against the backdrop of wider events. Napoleon controlled France and the Grande Armée was poised to conquer mainland Europe. England was seriously threatened with invasion and many young local men had enlisted to fight.

Bladon Castle

The local outcry was such that in order to take the heat out of the situation, a central block of rooms was hurriedly added behind the castle frontage and the Hoskins family moved in, thereby at least giving the folly a practical purpose. It was to prove a 'double whammy'. As a home, Bladon was far from ideal. The site lacked the basic necessity of water, so daily supplies had to be hauled uphill by mule. Added to that, the extra expense of making Bladon habitable put pressure on already stretched family finances.

Hoskins senior died in 1805. Abraham junior was a betting man and an ardent fan of field sports. Left in charge of the family's dwindling fortune he invested in coursing with characteristic over-the-top exuberance. The science of bloodlines was relatively new but gaining credence. Hoskins set up his own breeding pack of hounds, all with names beginning with 'H': Highlander, Hermes, High Flyer, Huntingdon, Hasty, Henrietta and so on. Hoskins's stud achieved widespread fame but despite huge sums of money lavished on his hobby, the results achieved in terms of prize money and competitions won were relatively modest.

Inevitably, the money drained away. In 1836, Hoskins was forced to sell Newton Hall to his neighbour, Lord Chesterfield, and move to a rather more modest villa-style house at Uttoxeter. Chesterfield rented the hall to Burton upon Trent brewer, William Worthington.

Ramada Jarvis Newton Park Hotel.

John Gretton

In the 1890s another local brewer, Richard Ratcliff, purchased the property. It was sold by the Ratcliff estate and became the Newton Park Hotel in 1966.

Ratcliff's brewing partner, John Gretton, accompanied him to Newton Solney and moved into Bladon Castle. By then the property was equipped with efficient pumps to supply water and, it is rumoured, had been given a decorative makeover by none other than influential arts and crafts designer William Morris.

The War Office requisitioned Bladon Castle during World War Two. Since 1972 it has been in private hands. As if still wary of public disapproval, Castle Wood provides a discreet veil guarding it from public view.

The Hoskins's star may have flared briefly but for a short time it blazed bright and left a lasting legacy. Many of Newton Solney's houses were built around 1800, as the village expanded under the patronage of Abraham Hoskins senior, using local bricks from John

Main Street, Newton Solney.

Hopkins's yard adjacent to Newton Hall. The Brickmakers Arms and an attractive row of former workers' cottages in Main Street are reminders of the mini-boom and the once flourishing brickworks.

As well as being High Bailiff of Burton upon Trent, Abraham senior's business interests extended to a directorship of the Burton Boat Company who leased shipping rights on the River Trent from Lord Paget. Stone for Newton Hall probably arrived at Newton Solney by sailing barge, delivered to a convenient port from quarries at Ancaster to be shipped upriver.

A tasteful marble tablet in Burton upon Trent's parish church of St Modwen commemorates the life of Abraham Hoskins senior. St Mary's, Newton Solney, has a memorial to Abraham junior, 'Late of this parish'.

Daydreams of sudden wealth are common. Perhaps finding that priceless antique in the attic; receiving an unexpected inheritance; coming up with a runaway new business idea; even winning the National Lottery jackpot. For most of us it will remain fantasy. But, if you do happen to strike lucky, remember Hoskins's folly. Do not underestimate the power of public opinion when it comes to spending your loot. What seems like a fun idea to impress the neighbours might just turn into a white elephant. Clearing up the mess could require one heck of a poop scoop.

6

BLESSED WERE THE CHEESEMAKERS

How local farmers led a rural revolution.

Agriculture in trouble. Powerful retailers dictating prices below the cost of production. Individual farmers played off against each other as they vie for business. Subsidies drying up, falling incomes, declining profitability and a government accused of turning its back on rural problems. An all too familiar clutch of soundbites but this was the situation 150 years ago. Price controls aimed at protecting domestic farmers had just been ended. Imported grain from the vast prairies of mid-western America undercut prices for homegrown crops. Newly developed refrigerated cargo ships allowed a flood of cheap meat and dairy products to cross the Atlantic.

Steam power and the coming of the railway opened up the prospect of big new markets for local dairy farmers. Milk trains ran overnight to Manchester and London. Until bulk tankers were introduced late in the 1970s, milk churns awaiting collection by the roadside were still a common sight in rural areas. Lifting these unwieldy heavy containers (imagine the average household bucket full of water and multiply by 10) required a practised technique.

The problems of the 19th century closely mirrored those of modern times. Milk prices barely covered costs. Small farmers in particular faced financial disaster. A fresh approach was desperately needed. It came through the combined visionary efforts of Lord Vernon of Sudbury Hall and the modernising ideas of Joseph Harding, an innovative farmer from the home of cheddar cheese, Somerset.

Lord Vernon travelled the world in his role as President of the Royal Agricultural Society. He took a keen interest in the latest farming technologies. Witnessing at first hand the economies of scale achieved in factory-style systems then emerging in the US he became convinced such methods offered a way forward for hard-pressed farmers in this country.

In England, a limited pooling of resources took place to produce the distinctive local cheeses of Cheshire and Somerset, and until the Reformation the big monastic houses had run large dairies. Essentially cheesemaking remained a small-scale operation carried out in individual farm dairies.

Cheese is one of the oldest manufactured foods. Until refrigerators became widely available, making cheese was the only way of preserving surplus milk. As with dairy farming generally, ewes' and goats' milk cheese probably came first. Although a demanding and laborious task, cheese and butter making was seen as women's work. If little Miss Muffet had been required to make her own curds and whey she would soon have developed a strong back and brawny forearms. Before Joseph Harding pioneered a more systematic approach, traditional cheese manufacturing techniques had hardly changed from prehistoric times. While the procedure was understood well enough the science behind it was not, and quality was very hit and miss.

At the start of the process, milk is prepared by gently heating it in a vat. Depending on the level of acidity and the type of cheese being made it is usually combined with a bacterial agent to 'kick start' fermentation. Adding a small amount of rennet, a naturally occurring enzyme found in calves' stomachs, causes the mixture to curdle and thicken into a smooth 'junket'. In mediaeval times lady's bedstraw, a feathery plant with clusters of tiny yellow flowers, was substituted if rennet was not available. Fairly common on well-drained grassland, this plant must contain a similar curdling enzyme. However, it also tended to give a slightly bitter tasting result.

When the junket is cut into small pieces the mixture separates leaving semi-solid curds and liquid whey. The whey is drained and the curds turned until ready to be compressed in a mould or 'chesset'. Early cheese presses were simply heavy stones laid on top of wooden moulds. By Victorian times tinned moulds were in use. These could be slotted into cast-iron presses fitted with screw threads, levers or spring mechanisms fixed to heavy-duty wooden frames.

With support from fellow committee member Edward Coke of Longford Hall, Lord Vernon outlined his plans to an enthusiastic audience of local farmers at a meeting of the newly formed Derby Agricultural Society. He proposed a co-operative venture to produce cheese employing the strict hygiene controls and scientific methods advocated by Joseph Harding. Shortly afterwards, on 4 May 1870, the first cheese factory in the country opened at Longford in south Derbyshire. Twenty-seven farmers with a combined herd of 500 cows supplied milk. The purpose-built timber building was cork-lined, aping the North American style. A raised platform ran along the front of the building to make loading and unloading easier. Blades powered by a water wheel automated the process of turning the curd. The first manager appointed was Cornelius Schermerhorn, an American with experience of factory cheese production.

The former cheese factory, Longford.

Good ideas travel fast and the venture was soon being copied across Derbyshire. In 1875, the Duke of Devonshire helped his tenant farmers to set up the Stilton creamery at Hartington. Among other new establishments were cheese factories in Egginton, Etwall and Marston Montgomery. In 1917 a factory was launched in Willington. By that time the factory system had all but taken over commercial cheese production and few farmers' wives continued to practice the old techniques.

Success was not universal. Some enterprises were simply too small to be viable. The Willington factory closed within a decade of opening and the buildings converted for other purposes. Others thrived and prospered. It was 1975 when the last round of Egginton Stilton from the dairy built beside the railway line close to Egginton Junction was sliced and eaten. The Hartington creamery still produces wonderful blue Stilton.

A century ago the cheese factories had proved a timely lifeline responsible for saving many local farmers from ruin. The original cheese factory at Longford is now converted into an unusual and historic private house.

In many ways a £16 million state-of-the-art dairy at Dove Valley Business Park, Foston, (opened in a blaze of publicity in May 2002 but belly up three months later) was an attempt to recreate the successes pioneered in 1870. The failure of Amelca plunged 150 local farmers, who together had pumped in significant sums of money to fund the venture, into deep trouble.

Milk churns awaiting collection, once a familiar sight.

Agriculture, particularly dairy farming, is once more in crisis. Co-operative ventures, local sourcing, diversification, organic produce and farmers' markets are just some of the ideas touted as potential routes to survival. Only time will tell if they can guarantee any sort of viable future in the long term. If ever an industry stood in need of men with the enthusiasm, influence and imagination of Lord Vernon and the inspiration of Joseph Harding, it is now.

7

CROSS PURPOSES

Enigmatic symbols of faith and commerce.

Christianity gained a precarious toehold in this country towards the end of the Roman occupation. Successive waves of pagan Anglo-Saxon invaders wore it away in the two centuries that followed the withdrawal of the legions. Re-conversion began with a somewhat reluctant papal emissary, Augustine, landing at Thanet in Kent in the year 597. When the Anglo-Saxons eventually embraced Christianity they did so wholeheartedly. Their God was a daily presence influencing every aspect of life. For those accused of misdeeds, trial by ordeal in the shape of grasping an iron bar red hot from a furnace, or plunging a hand into a cauldron of boiling water to pluck out a stone, was not the impossible lottery that it might appear from our contemporary perspective but was submission to infallible judgement by divine authority.

Before churches, free-standing crosses marked sacred sites. At these gospel stations priests would set up temporary altars and conduct Mass in the open air. Surviving examples of preaching crosses, and of memorial crosses from the early-mediaeval period, often contain both Christian and pagan symbols. Presumably an example of our forbears hedging their bets. Baptism into the new faith cannot have been an easy decision. Feast with Woden and your ancestors or enter the Kingdom of Heaven was the stark choice the Anglo-Saxons believed they faced. In this religious half-light it is hardly surprising that the symbols of faith became confused.

Our word church comes from the Celtic 'ciric', which translates as holy ground. It was as late as the 10th century when the term came to mean the building rather than the site on which it stood. Something of a church building boom began around this time and outdoor services held around a preaching cross became less common. Many early crosses have been lost and others badly mutilated, victims of assorted threats including Viking raids, the Reformation, Puritan extremism, simple neglect and exposure to the elements. Some fragments were recycled as building material. Following up a clue from a chance conversation with a drystone waller, I recently spotted a small section of cross built into a roadside wall near Birchover. Churches are the best places to look for the remains of early crosses. Two cross-shafts stand in the grounds of All Saints' Church, Bakewell, the largest

A cross-shaft from All Saints' Church, Bakewell.

of which stands two and a half metres high. On one side the crucifixion and Christian scenes are depicted, and another face shows Yggdrasil, the world tree of Scandinavian mythology, binding heaven, earth and hell in its branches and coiling roots. An eagle, a stag and a squirrel represent other pagan elements. Many more cross-shaft fragments line the south porch of the church.

One of the most complete crosses in Derbyshire stands in the churchyard of St Lawrence at Eyam.

A lucky survivor of rough treatment is a gritstone shaft now in the churchyard of All Saints, Bradbourne. This was found broken in two and being used as a squeeze stile in a field wall. A worn fragment of cross-shaft now outside St Thomas Becket Church, Chapel-en-le-Frith, was discovered in 1920 built into a local cottage.

A cross-shaft in the porch of St Wystan's Church, Repton, is decorated with finely carved human figures and foliage. A more important sandstone fragment, the 'Repton Stone' (now in Derby Museum), was discovered by archaeologists in 1979 at the foot of a pit originally dug to take a mediaeval scaffold pole. A snake with a human head is biting off the heads of two people on one side, while the other face shows a Saxon warrior on horseback. The warrior is believed to be Aethelbald, King of Mercia until his death in 757.

Saxon crosses, characterised by geometric patterns, animals, vine scrolls, knotwork and

The cross at Eyam is one of the most complete in Derbyshire.

The fragments of gritstone shaft at All Saints', Bradbourne.

interlace patterns, may be eighth, ninth or 10th century. Accurate dating of stonework is difficult and any attempt to do so necessarily involves a large element of guesswork.

Free-standing crosses were used for purposes other than as religious symbols although market crosses may have their origin in the preaching versions. Early traders exploited the footfall count at religious gatherings to sell their wares. With the arrival of officially-sanctioned markets founded

Buxton Market Cross.

Bonsall Cross, which dates from 1687.

by royal charter, crosses were erected to remind merchants of their moral duty not to cheat or short-change customers. Market crosses are later in date than preaching crosses but that does not always make them any easier to date. A 15th-century date is claimed for Buxton's market cross. Confusingly, the town did not receive a market charter until 1813.

Bonsall market cross, set on a circular platform of 15 steps, is inscribed with the date 1687.

Crosses were also used in mediaeval times as boundary markers. Champion Cross near Edale (see picture page 102) marked ward limits within the Royal Forest of the Peak in Norman times. Part of a cross head found in the River Wye and now at St Katherine's Church, Rowsley, has three arms radiating from a central boss, known as a 'Triquetra'. It is very similar to the Hexham frith stool, a Northumberland forest boundary cross.

Wooden crosses were typical of other parts of the country. Although a rare example turned up in 1954, buried beneath the ruined chancel of St Bertelin's Chapel, outside the present-day Church of St Mary, Stafford, they were particularly vulnerable to decay and few survive. The availability locally of millstone grit and sandstone has given Derbyshire a rich inheritance of stone crosses and cross shafts dating back to early times.

8

GREAT GATES AND STYLISH STILES

A fresh look at a functional and varied, but often overlooked, feature of our countryside.

'The rich man in his castle, the poor man at his gate.' By that measure I am off the scale, a man without even a gate never mind a castle. But, to continue the theme of Cecil Frances Alexander's hymn, if you want to see 'All things bright and beautiful, all creatures great and small' the place to be is the great outdoors, and you will not go far without coming across a gate or a stile. Since people began farming, around 5,000 years ago, gates and stiles have become a necessary and familiar part of our countryside. They are models of practical design with some interesting regional variations.

The first gates were made by simply slotting bars between a pair of upright posts to create a removable barrier. Swing gates, once known as 'wood and stone gates', developed where stone was used for field walls by fixing the ends of the crossbars to vertical beams and extending the ends of a hinge post to fit, top and bottom, into holes drilled in projecting stones. Iron pivot hinges were in use from Roman times, but metal was much too valuable for use to be widespread until the 18th century.

The gatepost at the hinge end takes the weight of the gate and is known as a 'harr' or sometimes the 'hanging post'. For economy, its partner upright, the 'head' or 'banging' post at the latch end, is often much lighter.

In the days when farmers asked a local carpenter to make their gates, with fixtures and fittings from the village smithy, there was wide variation in local styles. The best designs were soon copied. Of all gate patterns, the most universal is the 'five-bar' made of five horizontal rails or 'spanes' linked by vertical 'straps' and braced by a diagonal 'sword' from corner to corner. In southern counties of England the brace was usually cut to meet the top rail at its mid point in an inverted 'v'. Stronger, 'diamond bracing', with an upright 'v' bracing on the other side developed in the sheep country of East Anglia but is now common everywhere. In traditional Buckinghamshire gates the straps are cut off at the brace. Nowadays, most gates are

A 'creep hole', near Edale.

made of galvanised metal tubing but the basic tried and tested patterns of wooden field gates remain the same.

Double gates with a central fastening are useful for controlling the number of livestock passing through or for allowing large farm machinery access. Most gates are designed with animals or vehicles in mind. 'Kissing' or 'wicket' gates were used to allow people through while keeping livestock out.

In the Peak District, 'creep holes' can sometimes be seen in drystone walls. Their purpose was to keep cattle from straying while letting the small hornless old limestone sheep move from field to field.

Stiles are for people on foot. There are two basic types. Those you climb over and those you squeeze through. One of the cleverest designs is the 'clapper' stile with wooden rails that can be pushed down seesaw fashion and stepped over. These are rare but there is an example of one on a footpath through Snelston Park.

An example of a clapper stile, Snelston.

A typical Derbyshire step stile (left) and squeeze stile (above).

Perhaps the most intriguing stiles locally are a set of 11 'lyric' stiles set on a permissive footpath called the Staunton Ridgeway Walk. Posts have been attractively carved from oak trees felled on the Staunton Estate and each carries elements of a quotation. The path begins in the grounds of Staunton Harold Hall and leads northwards, skirting Dimminsdale nature reserve and out through Spring Wood and the Coppice on the east bank of Staunton Harold reservoir. You can make it a circular walk of about seven miles by continuing towards Breedon on the Hill and then cutting back on a public footpath across fields.

Walking northwards, the lyric stiles reveal a verse from Hilaire Belloc's *Dedicatory Ode* (1910):

> From quiet homes and first beginnings
> Out to the undiscovered ends,
> There's nothing worth the wear of winning
> But laughter and the love of friends.

Returning from the other direction, lines penned by John Blunt of the Staunton Harold Estate declare:

> Our paired legs stand to let your paired legs pass.
> We'll lead you where the grass is greener yet.

Now that is really putting on the stile.

One of the lyric stiles, Staunton Harold.

9
PIG TALES AND RABBIT HABITS

Pits, pigs, parades and mysterious climbing rabbits.

I like pigs. Perhaps the entertaining *Pinky and Perky* puppets of my childhood are to blame. The subject cropped up when I was looking into how mining communities have adapted and changed following pit closures. I find myself with mixed views about the passing of an industry once so dominant in Derbyshire. Records of coal mining in the south Derbyshire and north-west Leicestershire coalfield area stretch back to the early Middle Ages. No doubt the real origins are much earlier. Although pay, conditions, equipment and safety procedures improved, the coalface remained a demanding and dangerous place to work. Balancing the extraction of fossil fuels with environmental considerations has become a sensitive issue.

Little more than a century ago, the United Kingdom was the World's biggest producer of coal. At its peak, the Moira Colliery Company employed 700 men working in two pits. Next door at Donisthorpe, once acclaimed Britain's best pit, close to 400 men worked five seams. Within a generation the industry has shrunk to a fraction of its former size and has all but vanished locally. The National Forest's Discovery Centre now stands on the site of the former Rawdon Colliery. Nature, with a little assistance, has healed the visible scars on the landscape. Memories of a way of life run deeper.

The communities that grew up around the pits were closely knit, drawn together by ever-present hazards and shared experiences. People worked together and played together. In some cases hard-working committees have adapted former Miners' Welfare Clubs, Pigeon Associations and similar social activities, widening their appeal and thriving in the altered circumstances in which they find themselves. Inevitably, changes in lifestyle are reflected socially. Many of the fêtes and gala celebrations traditionally associated with mining communities no longer take place.

Moira may be a tiny village but in the past its annual parade and gala was a spectacular event. A large convoy of colourful floats, led by a brass band, wound slowly through the streets to congregate in a field. Everyone turned out to see the procession. And in this instance 'everyone' included the householders' pigs.

It is not so long ago that keeping a pig in a sty at the bottom of the garden was a common practice. The animals were often considered part of the family. In Moira, it

A photograph of the Moira Gala, taken sometime in the 1950s.

became the custom for people to dress up their pigs with coloured ribbons and to sit them outside on the garden wall where they could watch the parade go by. The ribbons used to decorate the pig were reckoned to bring good luck and were sold off, the proceeds helping to fund a village nurse service.

The days of keeping an individual pig passed but the Railway Inn in Ashby Road, Moira, took over from the Tollgate, popularly known as 'The Chain House', in maintaining the tradition into recent times. A piglet, dressed up for the gala day occasion, was put on the wall as the prize in a 'bowling for a pig' competition. At the end of the day, the highest scoring skittle player took the young porker home.

When Oakthorpe Colliery closed just over a decade ago there was a flurry of reports about tree-climbing rabbits. It was thought that a few rabbits had survived being trapped underground, with their offspring evolving front claws that equipped them to scale vertical walls. A similar spate of sightings followed the closure of the pit at Donisthorpe. Since then, despite a nocturnal habit and colouring that blends with the night shadows, a number of animals have been spotted in an area of land bounded by Moira, Donisthorpe and Willesley Wood. A Tree Rabbit Association has been set up to keep track of reported sightings.

The confinement of these unusual creatures in a relatively small triangular patch of land is reminiscent of the range of the Glis Glis of Buckinghamshire. These edible dormice, closer in size to a squirrel than our tiny native dormouse, were a favourite delicacy of the Romans. A century ago, half a dozen were brought to this country by Walter Rothschild and released in Tring Park. They bred and now thrive in a small area around Chesham Bois, moving into people's attics to hibernate for seven months of the year.

Rabbits hardly stop breeding long enough to sleep let alone hibernate. Their reproductive capacity is legendary. Each female is technically capable of producing up to eight litters of three to eight young a year. With rabbits becoming sexually mature at around six months it is easy to see the kick start any evolutionary adjustment gets, especially within a small group. The theory is that tree rabbits, isolated in murky subterranean conditions, rapidly adapted varied characteristics to produce a distinct species.

Television, travel and commuting has diluted dialects once so locally distinct you could tell in which village people lived. The tradition in 'Myra', I am reminded ('Are y'arkin?') is ('Let's be raight') to 'Put pig on't woll', the nurse was the 'noss' and the pub the 'Cheen Aase'.

10

BOXING CLEVER

The humble post box is well worth a closer look.

It may be the size of a domestic refrigerator and painted bright red but the post box rarely gets a second glance. We slide our correspondence in, maybe take a quick glance to confirm when the next collection takes place, and continue on our way. By and large we take for granted what has become such a familiar part of our street furniture. Perhaps that is a tribute to the quality of its design and functionality.

Royal Mail, the letters arm of the Post Office, has a history stretching back over 360 years. Henry VIII developed a prototype national message carrying service for his own personal use but it remained strictly a royal prerogative until Charles I, strapped for cash, opened up the network to paying customers in 1635.

Inns acted as collection points in the initial days of the mail. Post boys on horseback carried letters from town to town, a dangerous occupation with highwaymen a constant threat and road surfaces in a dilapidated state. One of Derbyshire's most feared 'gentlemen of the road' was known as Black Harry. A contemporary of Dick Turpin, Black Harry met the same fate and was hung at Wardlow Mires gibbet. A lane across Middleton Moor still carries his name.

The widespread introduction of turnpikes from the middle of the 18th century gave much of the responsibility for maintenance and new road building schemes to trusts set up especially to take on responsibility for main routes. Turnpike Trusts had powers to levy charges on users. It was an incentive for much needed capital investment. Travelling conditions improved as a result, halving journey times and enabling mail coaches to take over the carriage of letters and packages.

Mail coaches were exempt from road tolls. A warning blast on the post horn was sounded from a distance to give the tollhouse keeper time to throw open the barriers and allow the coach to pass at speed. Highway robbery was still a common enough occurrence and flintlock pistols became regulation issue for Post Office guards. From the 1830s, the railway began to supersede horse-drawn mail coaches.

In the early days, postal charges were invariably levied on receipt. Costs varied according to the distance involved and the number of sheets of paper contained in a message. It was an outdated and inefficient service wide open to fraud. Faced with increasing commercial demand change became essential. The man with the ideas was Rowland Hill, a kind of one-man independent think tank of his day. He submitted a pamphlet suggesting radical reforms to the then Prime Minister, Lord Melbourne. Hill's proposals were brought in progressively despite considerable opposition and became a model copied by postal services around the globe. His pioneering concepts included a single prepaid rate based on weight and the introduction in 1840 of the world's first and most famous postage stamp, the Penny Black. Hill went on to become secretary to the postmaster general and earned a knighthood.

Anthony Trollope, a clerk at the Post Office far better known today as the author of a sharply observed series of Victorian novels that include the *Chronicles of Barchester*, was the man responsible for the appearance of post boxes on our streets in the 1850s.

The first boxes, some in the now traditional red livery and others in a rich bottle green, had a vertical posting slot. There was no single design and a variety of hexagonal and circular fluted body shapes were produced. One company commissioned by the Post Office, Smith and Hawkes of Birmingham, famously misinterpreted the blueprint for an elaborate 'crown and cushion' style of box and built half a dozen 8ft tall examples before the mistake was noticed. In 1859, a decision was made to standardise boxes incorporating the now familiar horizontal aperture.

An example of a Penfold 'New Standard' post box, Buxton.

BOXING CLEVER

A Victorian wall-mounted post box, Sudbury.

J.W. Penfold revised this first nationally introduced design, in 1866. His 'New Standard' design was an elegant hexagonal box engineered by Cochrane and Company of Birmingham. A domed roof, decorated with a leaf pattern, was surmounted by a finial. A splendid example stands opposite Buxton's Opera House, and Stafford town centre boasts another.

As well as free-standing boxes in towns and cities, wall boxes began to appear in rural locations. Victorian wall boxes are still in use at Langton Junction, Pinxton; at the Boar's Head, Sudbury; in Hartington; and in Darley Dale and elsewhere. A projecting porch above the opening gave contents some protection from rain. By the end of the 19th century, small boxes were being attached to convenient lamp-posts and both slots and doors had been made larger to handle bigger packages. World famous Derby railway engineers, Andrew Handyside, produced many of the boxes used in the county.

The enterprising villagers of Horsley in Derbyshire built their own unique post box of local Coxbench stone in time for Christmas, 1896. Although no longer used it still stands at the corner of Church Street and French Lane.

The stone post box, Horsley.

Double-sized boxes with twin slots have been around for 100 years. Their use has gradually extended across the country but originally they were intended only for London to separate metropolitan deliveries from those destined for provincial addresses. The capital had been divided into 10 postal areas as far back as 1857 to help cope with the problem of sorting a mounting volume of mail.

Airmail began in 1911. In the 1930s a handful of blue boxes for international letters were placed in strategic sites. Demand grew at such a rate that these special boxes quickly became obsolete and airmail simply a regular part of the service.

Modern boxes, including the latest pole-mounted designs, have rotary dials that can be turned to show when the next collection is due to be made. Previously individual enamelled metal squares were dropped into slots and changed each time the box was emptied.

Royal monograms are an approximate indication of the age of individual boxes. Not surprisingly, most date from the last 50 years and wear the legend EIIR. But many earlier boxes can still be found. Keep a look out and, if you find one, send someone a postcard at least.

11

LORDING IT AT BRETBY

Every rank of nobility, from knights and barons to dukes and kings, has held the manor of Bretby. A mediaeval castle, gardens to rival the palace at Versailles; rebellion; siege; an eminent Victorian prime minister; a future Queen of England and the curse of Tutenkhamen, all feature in its history.

Bretby is a picturesque and tranquil village set on the south-west margin of Derbyshire. Its Scandinavian 'by' suffix reveals a name originating in the late-ninth century when a Danish army settled in central England. The rivers Trent and Dove marked a boundary between the Danelaw and Anglo-Saxon territory. For many years Bretby, or 'Place of the British', was a frontier settlement on a troubled border.

Before the Norman Conquest, Earl Algar, son of Lady Godiva and Earl Leofric of Mercia, held Bretby. After Algar died in 1062 Bretby would have passed either to his widow or one of his sons, Edwin or Morcar. By the time of the Domesday survey in 1086, Bretebi is among the possessions owned by William the Conqueror himself. Ownership later transferred to the de Kymba family, and in 1208 it was briefly in the hands of Ranulf de Blundevill, the powerful Earl of Chester.

For the early-mediaeval peasants of Bretby tilling the land, it can have mattered little which rapacious lord of the manor demanded their service. These were absentee landlords, rarely – if ever – seen, with vast estates spread around the country. That changed when Earl Ranulf sold Bretby to Stephen Segrave around 1209.

Segrave, newly appointed as justice itinerant for Derbyshire, chose to make Bretby his home and built himself a fashionable residence suitable for an ambitious young man on the make. The result was Bretby Castle, a spacious hall in the latest style with domestic buildings arranged around two internal courtyards and with a surrounding moat. Not a castle in the traditional sense of a draughty stronghold perched on an inaccessible rocky crag but a comfortable home, more Haddon Hall than Peveril of the Peak.

With a large manorial household to support, Bretby now needed other village necessities. Foundations were laid for a church just beyond the castle moat, and a watermill was built beside Repton Brook.

St Wystan's Church, Bretby.

The church, dedicated to St Wystan, became one of a number (there were others at Newton Solney, Foremark, Ingleby, Milton, Ticknall, Smisby, and Measham) in surrounding villages linked to the Augustinian priory at Repton. Uniquely among the early religious orders, the Augustinians, known as the Black Canons, did not lead a secluded life within monastic cloisters but worked in the community taking daily services, running schools and hospitals, and helping the poor and needy.

Stephen Segrave is a fascinating figure. A contemporary chronicler, Matthew Paris, claimed 'he came of no parentage'. While it is true that he was largely a self-made man who rose on merit and against the odds, he did have some advantages. Although his family were Saxon and of humble background in a Norman dominated, class-ridden society, his father Gilbert had prospered. Henry I, frustrated by the struggle to impose his will on truculent, independent-minded barons, decided on a deliberate policy of training a ministerial class to fill administrative positions. Gilbert, first of the family to adopt Segrave (after his home village in Leicestershire) as a surname, was clever and able enough to take advantage of the opportunity. Various public appointments followed. By the time of the Third Crusade, Gilbert was wealthy enough to contribute handsomely (400 marks, the equivalent of

£250,000 today) to Richard the Lionheart's fighting fund. In 1192 he was appointed joint sheriff of Leicestershire and Warwickshire, a position of power with endless scope for personal profit.

His father's success enabled Stephen to have the rare privilege of an education, most probably with the monks of Leicester Abbey, where he would also have learned the values of hard work and discipline. As a clerk, the crown of Stephen's head would have been shaved, a ceremonial tonsure in preparation for holy orders. He may even have planned a life of religious dedication. Instead of the Church, Stephen chose to make use of a sharp brain by becoming a lawyer. He was successful enough to attract the attention of King John, who had shared a similar monastic upbringing and was impressed by the young man's ability. Like John, Stephen was something of an outsider. He took no part in the baronial opposition faced by the king, and his support and loyalty were rewarded with lucrative and powerful public positions. In 1203, aged just 27, he was made constable of the Tower of London and in 1209 travelling justice for Derbyshire, a meteoric rise that enabled Stephen to buy the manor of Bretby. Under John's son and successor, Henry III, he landed the top legal job of chief justice, was made governor of several strategically important castles and served as sheriff of seven counties: Bedfordshire, Warwickshire, Leicestershire, Northamptonshire, Lincolnshire, Essex and Hertfordshire. Successive marriages to women from prominent, wealthy families, first Rose Despenser and then Ida Hastings, added to his standing. When Henry III left to campaign in France, the lord of the manor of Bretby was left in charge of England.

Stephan Segrave used his position to appoint his cronies to plum jobs. He and his clique showed little respect for feudal tradition and became increasingly unpopular with the established aristocracy. According to Matthew Paris, Stephen Segrave:

> …had the reputation of one of the
> chief men of the realm, managing
> the greatest affairs as he pleased.
> In doing whereof, he more minded
> his own profit than the common good.

The abuse of power led to violent disturbances. Civil war threatened. In 1233 arsonists targeted Segrave's property. To head off outright insurrection, King Henry brought charges against Segrave for 'wasting the King's treasure' and a warrant was issued. Stephen avoided arrest by seeking sanctuary at Leicester Abbey. Peace was restored and a deal negotiated. Segrave paid a fine of 1,000 marks, was forgiven by King Henry and reappointed chief counsellor. Honour restored, Stephen left public life soon afterwards, retiring to end his days as a humble canon at Leicester Abbey, leaving Bretby to his son Gilbert.

Gilbert Segrave was made governor of Bolsover Castle and also of Kenilworth Castle. In 1242, the year after his father's death, he was appointed justice for all the royal hunting forests south of the River Trent.

Gilbert's heir, Nicholas, supported Simon de Montfort against Henry III and led the first charge at the Battle of Lewes in 1264. As virtual ruler of England, De Montfort made Nicholas a peer. A year later, defeat at the Battle of Evesham left Nicholas wounded and outlawed, hiding out with the remnants of the rebel army in the Fens surrounding Ely. Temporarily, Bretby was forfeit to the Crown, but Nicholas was a good soldier and was offered the chance to redeem himself in the King's service. Fighting beside the future Edward I on crusade in Wales and in Ireland, he not only earned a full pardon but also regained the title of 1st Lord Segrave.

John Segrave inherited his father's fighting spirit, serving with distinction against the Welsh and as the king's lieutenant in Scotland where he invented the 'Segrave' siege-engine, a type of trebuchet using a counterpoise mechanism to launch rocks at a target. In 1301, John was granted a licence to add battlements to Bretby Castle, more as a trendy fashion statement than for serious military purpose. No shots were ever fired in anger at Bretby.

John was captured twice during the Scottish campaign of 1302. The first time he was ransomed and on the second occasion daringly rescued by Robert Nevill, the 'Peacock of the North'. In 1305 John Segrave was one of the judges who condemned William Wallace to be hung, drawn and quartered.

Fighting alongside his older brother in Scotland was Nicholas. Nicholas Segrave quarrelled with John Cromwell, a fellow officer. Forbidden to fight a duel while on campaign, Nicholas and Cromwell withdrew their men and left secretly to settle their differences in France. On his return to Dover, Nicholas was arrested and summoned to appear before Parliament. He pleaded guilty, knowing the only possible verdict was death. In the event, his sentence was remitted to imprisonment. He was later released and pardoned when Edward II succeeded to the throne in 1307.

In 1314 the Segrave brothers were back in Scotland, this time with Edward II, and were on the losing side against Robert the Bruce at Bannockburn. Once again, John was captured but released in an exchange of prisoners negotiated by his son, Stephen.

Stephen followed in his great-grandfather's footsteps as constable of the Tower of London. Understandably angry after rebel Roger Mortimer, Earl of March, escaped during Stephen's watch (in exile Mortimer became Queen Isabella's lover and was destined to depose the King) Edward II ordered John, Stephen and Stephen's teenage son John to defend England's interests in France. It was almost as good as a death sentence. An epidemic was raging in Gascony and Stephen and his father both died. John junior survived and returned to Bretby as 4th Lord Segrave. His marriage to Margaret, daughter of the Earl of Norfolk and granddaughter of Edward I, allied the Segraves to the Plantagenets. John fought in Scotland and France. In 1346 he left for France from Portsmouth and took part in Edward the Black Prince's famous victory at Crécy, where an outnumbered English army cut down the flower of French aristocracy.

Imagine Lord Segrave marching out from Bretby, lion rampant banner fluttering in the breeze, accompanied by eight knights in burnished armour with their squires, and perhaps

The possible tomb of Sir John, 4th Lord Segrave, Gaddesby.

80 men-at-arms and archers recruited locally. When John Segrave died in 1353 with no male heir, ownership of Bretby passed to John Mowbray, husband of eldest daughter Elizabeth Segrave.

An elusive trail of clues led me to the tomb of an unknown knight in St Luke's Church, Gaddesby, Leicestershire, that I think may be Sir John, 4th Lord Segrave. So far, positive identification has not been possible. Lady Margaret lived on at Bretby Castle until her death in 1399, remarrying first Sir Walter Manny, another Crécy veteran, and then Thomas de Erdington.

Victory at Crécy presaged the dawn of a new age of chivalry inspired by Arthurian legend. The prestigious Order of the Garter was founded as Edward III sought to recapture the spirit of chivalry, with Windsor as his Camelot and 26 hand-picked nobles representing the Knights of the Round Table. Lady Margaret was at the joust in Lichfield to see Sir Walter Manny invested as a Knight of the Garter in 1359. In 1384, their daughter Anne became one of the first Ladies of the Garter when she was invested alongside Anne of Bohemia, Queen Consort of England.

Eight generations of Mowbrays held Bretby, but after the death of Lady Margaret,

Seal of John, 2nd Lord Segrave: garbs (sheaves) and lion rampant.

Seal of Lady Margaret Segrave: angel crest above the arms of Segrave, Plantagenet and Manny.

Bretby Castle was no longer a main residence. When the last of the line, Thomas, Duke of Norfolk, Earl of Nottingham and Earl Marshall of England died childless around 1480, Bretby passed to a cousin William, Viscount Berkeley. William was followed by his brother Maurice who was summarily disinherited for marrying a commoner whose father was 'in trade' in Bristol. It was 70 years before the extensive Berkeley family estate was fully restored. By then, Bretby Castle was neglected, run down and rented out.

When Sir Thomas Stanhope of Shelford, a Trentside village in Nottinghamshire, bought the Bretby estate in 1585 from the Marquess of Berkeley, it was an investment in securing the future for his family. He was 45. Bretby Castle, now almost four centuries old, was in a ruinous state. In any case, the castle was leased to Thomas Duport until 1610 and rented out to sitting tenants John and Mary Mee.

It was Thomas's grandson, Sir Philip Stanhope, who took possession of Bretby in 1610. He immediately commissioned a new house, designed it is said by a young Inigo Jones, choosing a site half-a-mile south-west of the old castle, whose ancient battlemented walls were levelled and plundered for stone. The result was a magnificent mansion, second only to Chatsworth in magnificence, surrounded by a deer park, lakes and French-style formal gardens based on those at the Palace of Versailles complete with fountains, groves and labyrinths.

Sir Philip's flamboyant lifestyle upset many of his peers. His Shelford neighbour, Sir John Holles, complained he was 'a perpetual dishonour to the King and all the nobility'. There were brushes with the law, including two indictments for illegal sexual practices. He was cleared on both counts and continued to serve as a magistrate. In 1628, he was created Earl of Chesterfield.

Philip gave no indication in his early years of strong political views or moral principles. With civil unrest brewing in 1639 he excused himself from a summons to meet King Charles at York pleading 'extremity of weakness' from which he 'doubted he would recover'. But when the Civil War broke out three years later he proved himself a steadfast Royalist. Bretby was fortified in the name of the king and a garrison raised for its defence.

In December 1642, Bretby was besieged. Outnumbered, Philip abandoned his wife Anne and set off for Lichfield. According to the gloss put on what happened next by the Parliamentarian commander, the officers in charge asked the countess to buy off the soldiers to stop them ransacking the house. When she refused, they offered to lend her the money, an offer she turned down and Bretby Hall was looted. A few weeks later, Philip Stanhope surrendered and spent the rest of the conflict under house arrest in London. His

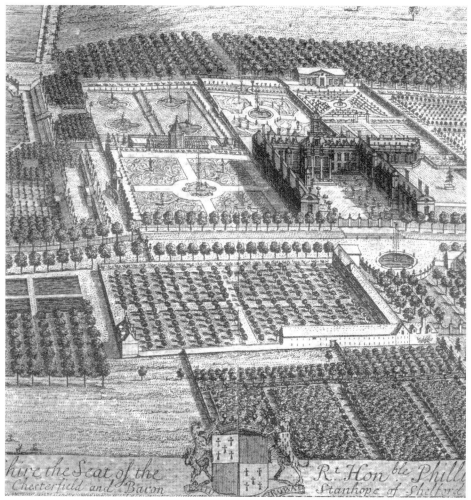

The early 17th-century gardens, Bretby Hall.

fine mansion at Bretby was lost as the spoils of war and his estates sequestered. Countess Anne was forced to tighten her bodice and live on an allowance of £5 per week. By the time the war ended, three of the earl's sons had died in the Royalist cause.

When the old earl died, still in prison, in 1656, it was left to his grandson Philip to reclaim Bretby. Philip was travelling abroad after prudently quitting an academy in Paris following a duel. Returning to England, he refused an offer of marriage to one of Oliver Cromwell's daughters and a military commission with the Commonwealth. Instead he embarked on a series of high profile affairs and was soon in trouble again for duelling. In 1659, Philip spent time in the Tower of London for his part in a Royalist conspiracy. On his release, he killed a man in a dispute over the price of a horse and fled abroad. But the political climate was changing. At the Dutch court, Philip met Charles Stuart and obtained a pardon. Within months, Charles was on his way to be crowned king of England. Philip was at his side. Stanhope loyalty was rewarded. Bretby was returned and Philip appointed lord chamberlain to Queen Catherine.

Philip Stanhope married the beautiful Lady Elizabeth Butler and sent her to live at Bretby to escape the amorous attentions of the King's brother James, Duke of Hamilton. It was rumoured that Hamilton pursued her to Derbyshire. A servant sent by Lady Elizabeth met the duke and promised to lead him to a secret rendezvous. Instead, the duke was led in circles around the Bretby Estate until he was totally disoriented, cold, tired, wet and dirty.

When Elizabeth died in 1665, Philip retired from court and devoted himself to life at Bretby, putting his energies into restoring the house and gardens. Four years later, he remarried Elizabeth Dormer, daughter of the Earl of Carnarvon. When she died after a miscarriage in 1677, Philip planted a Cedar of Lebanon seedling, one of the first in this country. As the majestic tree grew so did a legend that when a branch fell it foretold the death of a member of the family.

The 3rd Earl succeeded in 1713 and enjoyed the life of a country gentleman. After touring Europe and becoming a Tory MP at 21, his son and heir Philip Dormer Stanhope found Bretby less than exciting, describing his home in a letter as 'the seat of horror and despair'. After inheriting Bretby in 1726 as the 4th Earl of Chesterfield, he made a name for himself in the House of Lords as a witty speaker and was entrusted with several important and sensitive diplomatic missions. Given his aversion to the country life it was not surprising that he chose to live in London, reviving the dwindling Stanhope bank balance by marriage to the wealthy 40-year-old Duchess of Kendal, Petronilla von der Schulenberg, illegitimate daughter of George I.

Philip Dormer Stanhope is best remembered for a series of letters, later published, giving guidance on how to behave in fashionable society that were written to his son from an extra-marital relationship. Samuel Johnson caustically observed that the letters 'teach the morals of a whore, and the manners of a dancing master'.

Neglected by the 4th Earl, the grand mansion at Bretby fell into decay. When house and title passed to his cousin Philip in 1773 the house was beyond saving. A new hall was begun, designed by Jeffrey Wyatville. The old formal gardens, no longer fashionable, were ripped out and replaced by parkland reflecting a more natural landscape. Revival of the estate continued under the 5th Earl.

Bretby Hall.

The 6th Earl completed the house and added a racecourse in the park. Modern Bretby village grew up around the estate. A school was provided for local children. Bretby Hall played host to high society, and Prime Minister Benjamin Disraeli and the future Queen Mary were both regular guests. Daughter Evelyn married the Earl of Carnarvon at Westminster Abbey. After the death of the 5th Earl, Disraeli proposed to his widow, Countess Anne, but was rejected. A memorial plaque in St Wystan's Church, rebuilt by Anne in 1878, records:

> **In memory of Benjamin Disraeli, Earl of Beaconsfield**
> The foremost man of his age. Eminent in Letters,
> in Council, in debate. A statesman far-seeing
> and sagacious, a Patriot zealous for his Country's
> honour. A devoted servant of the Queen, by whom
> he was trusted, honoured and mourned.
> This tablet is erected by Anne Elizabeth, Countess
> of Chesterfield a record of a much prized friendship
> and a lasting regret.

When Anne died in 1885, the house passed to her grandson, George, 5th Earl of Carnarvon. Howard Carter visited Bretby on many occasions as he and Carnarvon planned an expedition to investigate the treasures of ancient Egypt. To help finance the venture, Bretby was sold to J.D. Wragg of Swadlincote. The herd of 200 deer were culled and part of the 450-acre park turned over to agriculture.

Six years later Carter and Carnarvon set the archaeological world alight with the discovery of Tutenkhamen's tomb. When Carnarvon died shortly afterwards amid talk of the mummy's curse, people visited Bretby to see if the ancient Cedar of Lebanon had shed a bough.

The famous Cedar of Lebanon, Bretby Hall.

SEGRAVE OF BRETBY

Hereward (b.c.1114)

Gilbert Hereward Segrave (1144–1202)

Stephen (1176–1241) m. 1. Rose Despenser m. 2. Ida Hastings

Gilbert (1201–54) m. Annabel Chaucombe (1210–78)

Nicholas 1st Lord Segrave (1238–1295) m. Maud Lucy (b.1239)

John (1256–1325) m. Christiana Pless (d.c.1330)
2nd Lord Segrave

Nicholas (d.1322)

Stephen (d.1325) m. Alice Warner
3rd Lord Segrave

John (1306–53) m. Margaret Brotherton (1320–99)
4th Lord Segrave

Elizabeth (b.1338) m. John, Lord Mowbray

STANHOPE OF BRETBY

Thomas Stanhope (1540–96) m. Margaret Port of Etwall

John Stanhope (c.1578–1609) m. 2. Cordell Allington

Philip Stanhope, 1st Earl of Chesterfield m. 1. Catherine Hastings m. 2. Anne Ferrers
(1584–1656)

Henry Stanhope (d.1634) m. Catherine Wotton

Philip Stanhope, 2nd Earl m. 1. Anne Percy m. 2. Elizabeth Butler m. 3. Elizabeth Dormer
(1633–1713))

Philip, 3rd Earl (d.1726) m. Elizabeth Savile

Philip Dormer, 4th Earl (1694–**1773**) m. Petronilla von der Schulenberg

BY ADOPTION

Philip, 5th Earl (1755–1815) m. 2. Henrietta Thynne

George, 6th Earl (1805–66) m. Anne Weld-Forester (1802–85)

George (7th Earl) (1831–71)

Eveleyn m. Henry Herbert, 4th Earl Carnarvon

George, 5th Earl Carnarvon (1866–1923)

Derbyshire County Council bought Bretby Hall for use as an orthopaedic hospital in 1926. The once noble Cedar of Lebanon, almost certainly the oldest surviving tree of its kind in the country, barely alive and held together by chains, was reduced to a stump in 1954 and blew down completely in a gale shortly afterwards.

Now the hospital too has closed. Bretby Hall has been converted into 29 luxury apartments looking out over parkland, flanked by modern domestic properties. The former village school is a private house, the Segrave's mediaeval castle a faint, shadowy footprint on Castle Field and Bretby village a haven of tranquillity. No casual visitor would guess what freight of history this picturesque place carries.

12

THE TIME OF DAY

Taking time out to track down some fascinating sundials.

In the beginning there was light and we have worshipped it ever since. Measuring our day by the apparent progress of the sun across the sky. Noon marks the meridian when the sun is highest. The interval until it crosses this point again is our 24-hour day. Except that it is not exactly 24 hours. A few seconds either way slip irretrievably behind the cushion of time's settee in the process. Close enough for our ancestors but not for our modern world.

The basis for standard time zones, introduced by international agreement in 1883 to iron out the discrepancies in the solar cycle, is 'Mean' Time. It seems an apt phrase. Solar time sounds much more natural and somehow less demanding. We have taken time, tamed and regularised it, and strapped it on our wrist. But who really is the servant and who the master?

An example of a scratch dial.

THE TIME OF DAY

Time is an intriguing concept. I was amused recently when a telephone caller from New Zealand opened the conversation by enquiring 'Is it yesterday?'. Before digital watches and mechanical clocks were invented the shadow cast by the sun was used to calculate time. Sundials were used in ancient Egypt and receive Biblical mentions in Isaiah and the Book of Kings. They have a fair claim as the first gadgets.

Despite the unpredictability of sunshine locally, we have some fascinating examples, the earliest dating back to Anglo-Saxon times. They were used to indicate the times when markets were officially allowed to trade or when church services were due to begin. Some are finely carved but most surviving dials are plain and uncomplicated and known as 'scratch' dials. Later models became more sophisticated and are capable of precise interpretation.

On scratch dials a central hole is all that usually remains to show where the 'gnomon' – a protruding peg that cast the shadow – once fitted. Incised lines indicating the hours radiate from this hub. As you look at a dial, morning hours are on the left of the noon line and afternoon is to the right. Generally, older dials have fewer lines. The Anglo-Saxons were not particularly concerned with measuring hourly units, dividing their day into the broader bands of morning tide, evening tide and so on.

Surviving church Mass dials have often been rescued from their original positions on south facing outside walls and resited during restoration or rebuilding. They are easy to overlook. A weathered early scratch dial is now incorporated in one of the chancel buttresses of St Lawrence's Church, North Wingfield.

At Stanton-by-Dale, an intriguing dial, probably dating back to the 13th-century origins of St Michael and All Angels, is set above the south doorway of the church. It is protected now by a porch that was a later addition. A tiny central circle, set inside a segmented outer rim that may be intended to represent the sun, has lines at 9am, noon, 3pm and 6pm.

Sundials come in two basic designs. Horizontal dials are the most common. These have a gnomon set at an angle equal to the exact latitude of the location. On vertical, wall-mounted models, this angle has to be calculated to match the co-latitude, the difference between site latitude and 90 degrees.

Sundials are frequently found in churchyards. Even when clocks began to replace them as timepieces they remained useful for resetting cumbersome and less reliable mechanical devices in the days before the Greenwich 'pips' time signal. Contemplating time attracts poets and philosophers and many sundials have associated individual mottoes or verses.

The complex sundial of St Lawrence's, Eyam.

At St Thomas Becket in Chapel-en-le-Frith the dial reminds us that *Tempus Fugit*. Others have less familiar messages. One of the finest and most complex dials to be found anywhere adorns St Lawrence's Church at Eyam, the gift of churchwardens William Lee and Thomas Froggat in 1775. The Latin tag exhorts us to encourage spirit and wisdom: *Induce Animum Sapientum*. In addition to indicating local time a curving graph on the face shows noon at various locations around the world, including Mecca, Constantinople, Quebec and Mexico. For those with sufficient expertise to decipher the dial it also contains a wealth of astrological and astronomical information.

A more traditional horizontal dial, made by Derby clockmaker John Whitehurst in 1767, now stands on a tall pillar in St Leonard's churchyard, Thorpe. Viewing for most requires standing on tiptoe or being on horseback.

A pillar dial at St Anne's, Baslow, is one of a number of visible memorials in the area recalling Lt Col Edward Wrench, who became the village doctor in 1862 after active service

A pillar dial, St Leonard's, Thorpe.

as an army surgeon in Empire hotspots such as the Crimea and India. At St John's, Tideswell, the base supporting the pillar on which a dial is set shows evidence of being the recycled remains of a mediaeval churchyard cross.

It was the coming of the railways that made standardisation of time necessary. In the solar cycle

A pillar dial, St Anne's, Baslow.

The pillar dial at St John's, Tideswell, may sit on the remains of a mediaeval churchyard cross.

exact noon varies with locality. Midday in Buxton occurs a couple of minutes later than in Chesterfield. Not exactly jet lag proportions but enough to play havoc with the schedules on long-distance cross-country journeys. The convenience of standard time has made the sundial redundant. But although mere functional usefulness has passed they remain absorbing and decorative objects, well worth passing the time of day with when you come across one.

13

GREEN FOR DANGER

An Arthurian tale with local links.

In northern Europe we have always felt the need to brighten up the dark days of midwinter. In pagan times, Yule logs were lit using an ember carefully preserved from the previous year, marking the start of a 12-day period of celebration and feasting. One seasonal tale told around the hearths of the great halls of mediaeval England was that of Sir Gawain and the Green Knight. A single precious copy of this 14th-century manuscript exists at the British Museum.

It is Yuletide at the court of King Arthur. As the court makes merry a gatecrasher in the shape of the Green Knight arrives to spoil the revels. He challenges any knight bold enough the chance of a free swing on condition that should he survive his attacker must present himself at the Green Chapel and submit to a return blow. As his companions dither before the taunts of this threatening apparition it is left to Gawain to front up. He steps forward, and taking the intruder's own battleaxe lops off his head with a single stroke. Instead of keeling over the Green Knight tucks his severed head beneath his arm and departs.

Somewhat reluctantly, Gawain sets out to keep his part of the bargain. The quest to find the Green Chapel takes him into unknown country far from Camelot. There are adventures and encounters along the way. After a long journey dogged by weather that would disgrace a Bank Holiday, Gawain arrives at Castle Hautdesert, home of Sir Bertilak. Here Gawain learns he is close to his goal. The Green Chapel is not far away and Bertilak promises to show him the way but first he has a few days sport planned. In the meantime he offers him hospitality with a side bet to make the stay more interesting. While Gawain rests ahead of his ordeal, his host intends to hunt. At the end of each day the two will exchange their respective catches.

Once Bertilak has left the castle, his attractive wife attempts to seduce the visitor. Gawain is one of Arthurian legend's more lusty knights, not usually needing much encouragement to unbuckle his codpiece, and the lady is beautiful, but beyond a single chaste kiss he is a perfect gentleman and politely refuses her advances. That evening Bertilak returns with a deer. As promised he makes a present of his catch to Gawain who gives him a kiss in return.

Next day, Bertilak again rides out. His wife once more tries to tempt Gawain and fails, but this time they kiss twice. When Bertilak returns with a boar he receives two kisses from his guest. A repeat performance on the third day leads to three kisses and the gift of a green sash. Bertilak's wife assures Gawain that if he wears it beneath his armour its magic properties will protect him from the Green Knight's axe.

After a less successful day in the forest, Bertilak has only a fox to show for his efforts. Nevertheless he hands it to Gawain who kisses his host three times but keeps quiet about the magic sash.

On the fourth day, Bertilak leads Gawain to the Green Chapel and his appointment with the Green Knight. Gawain bravely bows his head before the fearsome figure. Twice he flinches, pulling back to let the axe whistle harmlessly by. The third time he holds still but as the axe falls it merely grazes his neck.

The whole adventure is then revealed as an illusion set up by the sorceress, Morgan Le Fay, a practical test of the spirit and chivalry avowed by those with seats around the Round Table. Gawain's blood is spilled because he failed to own up about the sash but his life is spared because, despite his all too human lapses, overall he has acted with honour and courage. It is his integrity in dealing with temptation that saves Gawain not some superstitious nonsense about a strip of cloth tied around his waist.

Does the beheading of a 'green' knight symbolise the winter solstice? Is his survival an affirmation of life and the cycle of rebirth? The poem's rich imagery and symbolism is open to many allegorical interpretations.

For all the fanciful elements of magic and fantasy much of the story is realistic. Gawain's armour is described in fine detail. Courtly etiquette, particularly the exchanges between Gawain and the lady of Castle Hautdesert, is described with precision. Our anonymous poet sets his tale against a background that would be familiar to a cultured audience of the day.

Gawain and the Green Knight was written around 1380, at the same time as Geoffrey Chaucer was redefining English literature. Stylistically it has been called old fashioned. The poem's rhythm and metre have more in common with the Anglo-Saxon epics and Viking sagas than the polite lyric verse rhymes introduced by the Normans. But this was an age when most texts were religious and in Latin. English was only just reasserting itself over French as the language of court and of administration. Seen in that context, our poet's plundering of the fertile word-hoard that was England's Anglo-Saxon inheritance seems absolutely forward-looking and of its period. *Gawain and the Green Knight*'s 3,000 lines

Lud's Church, Staffordshire. Was this the Green Chapel from the legend of Gawain and the Green Knight?

follow a tightly structured format. It is a performance poem intended for reading aloud. But where might it have found its audience?

There are clues. There was no such thing as standard English in the 14th century. The poem is written in dialect. Experts generally agree the language used places it firmly in the north midlands. Dominant in the area at the time was John of Gaunt, Duke of Lancaster. John effectively ruled England and kept a court at Tutbury Castle unrivalled outside of London. A patron of the arts, John of Gaunt supported Chaucer financially. He entertained lavishly when in residence at Tutbury and organised the ragbag 'histriones' who turned up for the annual minstrels's court into a more professional outfit.

Writing was a rare skill in mediaeval England and mostly confined to religious communities. This has led to a suggestion that the author of *Gawain* was a monk. If so, a powerful patron would have been necessary in order for the writer to get away with the superstitious elements of the story.

The Green Chapel has been associated with the 20m deep, sunless ravine known as Lud's Church, a narrow rocky gorge hidden high on the wooded slopes above the River Dane in north Staffordshire. Mysterious and atmospheric, it would make an ideal setting likely to be known to a local audience.

Radio, film and television have largely taken over the storyteller's role. A trilogy of films based on Tolkien's *Lord of the Rings* were recent blockbuster hits. It is interesting perhaps to reflect that Tolkien drew much of his inspiration from early English literature. His version of *Gawain* was published in 1927.

14

COCK AND BULL STORY

Blood sports have long been surrounded by controversy.

Opponents said it was cruel and barbaric. Supporters claimed a ban was an erosion of ancient freedoms. Some believed it was an attack on individual liberties partly motivated by class hatred. They pointed to centuries of tradition and vowed to continue, even flouting the law of the land if necessary. Bull baiting, popular since Roman times, was once widespread. Often taking place at annual wakes or fairs or as part of a special celebration. Guests at a wedding reception held in Darley Dale, Derbyshire, in 1798 were entertained by two baiting sessions.

Typically, a 5m tether secured to either a post or a ring confined the bull. Horns were blunted or sheathed. Sometimes pepper was blown up the beast's nostrils to ginger it up for the fight. Bulldogs, bred for their aggressive qualities, were then set upon the creature one at a time ('one dog one bull' was the rule said to ensure fair play!). Dog owners circled the action ready to catch their pet if it should be tossed out of the ring. Once a tenacious dog had a good hold it was unlikely to let go until it had bitten through whatever its jaws were clamped around.

Most towns held baiting spectacles. An interesting variant took place at Tutbury each August. A bull had its horns and tail cut off and its body smeared with soap. It was then set loose and chased, and after capture it was baited in High Street. In 1778, the vicar of Tutbury, with support from Lord Vernon of Sudbury Hall, successfully petitioned the Earl of Devonshire to end the annual bull-running because of the drunken revelry and general rowdiness that accompanied the event. The baiting part of the entertainment, however, was allowed to continue.

Most baiting was associated with market places or public houses. The large crowds attracted were good for trade. Owners paid a fee to enter their dog and the beef was sold afterwards making it a potentially profitable exercise. Sometimes a group would pool their resources to buy a bull and stage a co-operative event.

Bear baiting, reserved for special occasions (bears disappeared in this country during the 11th century and had to be imported, making them expensive), were even more of a spectator magnet. An old folksong accuses the inhabitants of Uttoxeter of 'selling the church bible to buy a town bear'.

During civil unrest at the time of the 1715 Jacobite uprising, religious nonconformists suffered the consequences of siding with the Government over the Hanoverian succession. In Burton upon Trent, a bull was taken – most probably from outside the nearby Bear Inn in Horninglow Street – to the Congregational Meeting House in High Street (later the site of the Congregational Chapel and now the Riverside Church). Here the unfortunate creature had its tail cut off and its ears cropped. When the troublemakers tried to push the maddened bull through the doors of the Meeting House the crazed animal broke free. Pursued by the mob, the bull raced off along High Street before turning into the Market Place and crashing into St Modwen's Church where a service was underway. *The Flying Post*, a national pro-Government journal, reported three dead and several crushed or gored before order was restored.

Bull baiting was predominantly a working class indulgence. All classes pursued cockfighting. Henry VIII established a cockpit at Whitehall. James I and Charles II were both keen followers of the sport and it was frequently referred to as the 'Royal Diversion'. Inns were the chief venues for cockfighting, though enough of the gentry used their drawing rooms for furniture makers to offer specially designed wooden chairs with arms at shoulder height circling out from the top rail of a narrow back rest. Burton upon Trent had a cockpit at the rear of the Vine Inn, Horninglow Street. There was a cockfighting loft in the attics of a property on the corner of School Lane, Sudbury. At Ashbourne, the Blackamoor's Head (now part of the Green Man and Black's Head Royal Hotel) was cockfighting central for the Derbyshire Dales area. Burton brewer William Sketchley published a manual called *The Cocker*, covering the complicated rules and procedures involved in matches.

Birds were matched by weight and fought three-minute rounds supervised by a referee. A count of 10 was allowed for birds to recover between particularly severe exchanges (all practices later adopted by boxing). Fights were to the death. Vicious spurs of bone or metal were often fitted to birds's legs. A 'main' of up to 39 cocks (it was always an odd number) was a normal entry for a tournament. Each individual contest carried prize money and gambling for high stakes accompanied matches.

The cockshy was a traditional Shrove Tuesday event for young men. A cockerel was tied to a stake and youths took turns to throw a stick at it from a distance of 22 yards (an old measure of a chain equal to the distance between the wickets on a modern cricket pitch). The idea was to knock the bird down and retrieve your stick before it recovered to win the cock.

COCK AND BULL STORY

In the country at large there was rising opposition to the bloodthirsty exhibitions of baiting and cockfighting, but Parliament was divided. A proposal to ban bull baiting was narrowly defeated in 1802. The thin end of the wedge came 20 years later. MP Richard Martin (widely known by his nickname of 'Humanity Dick') steered the first Animal Protection Bill through Parliament. Two years after the Act was passed a campaigning group, the Society for the Prevention of Cruelty to Animals (SPCA) was launched. The 1822 Act was not the best-framed legislation. What constituted cruelty under the Act was subject to interpretation and legal challenge. Nevertheless, a number of successful prosecutions followed. Public opinion was also hardening. In 1834, the vicar of St James's Church, Bonsall, paid a guinea to buy a bull and save it from being baited. A year later, Parliament passed a much more definitive law specifically prohibiting the baiting of both bulls and bears. For bull baiting it meant the law had come full circle. Based on the belief that torture tenderised, many towns (Chesterfield among them) had by-laws prohibiting the killing of a bull unless it had been baited first. Transgressors faced a hefty fine.

A typical bull ring, Eyam.

The tethering post in the market place, Newark.

Diehard enthusiasts vowed to defy the ban and continue their sport, but those who flouted the law risked fairly severe punishment. A prosecution by the SPCA in Suffolk resulted in 12 men being fined a total of £43. Seven of the group refused – or were unable – to pay and served two months in prison with hard labour. In an indication of the public mood, Queen Victoria gave her blessing to the SPCA in 1840, allowing it to add 'Royal' to its name.

Bear baiting re-invented itself as bear dancing and continued as an occasional street entertainment into the 20th century. Cockfighting was outlawed altogether in 1849. Driven underground, it continued at secret locations but was much reduced. Bull rings, relics of the past, can still be seen at Eyam, Foolow and Snitterton.

A tethering post remains in the corner of the cobbled Market Place at Newark. Public houses with Bull, Bear and Cock in their name may owe their name to a previous association. We still occasionally take a 'cockshy' at things, though once popular phrases such as 'to live like fighting cocks' i.e. in the lap of luxury, have fallen out of common use. Cock-a-leekie soup is supposed to have arisen from a Scots and north country tradition of having a pan of vegetables on the boil during a cockfight and tossing the loser into the mix. Of course, that may just be a 'cock-and-bull' story. Far-fetched tales that stretch credulity are said by some to have gained the epithet because a large number of classical fables involve the two animals.

An alternative theory is that the saying originated at Stony Stratford where the Cock and the Bull, two coaching inns, stand next door to each other on old Watling Street. It is claimed that travellers lodging overnight entertained themselves by trying to outdo each other in telling tall stories that were carried between the taverns. I rather like that version. Sounds like a good game. Then again, I might have cocked up.

15

SECRETS OF THE FOREST

Mediaeval hunting reserves.

Referring to the setting up of royal hunting forests after the Norman Conquest, the *Anglo-Saxon Chronicle* says of King William:

> He made great protection for the game
>
> And imposed laws for the same,
>
> So that those who slew hart or hind
>
> Should be made blind.
>
> He preserved the harts and boars
>
> And loved stags as much
>
> As if he were their father.

Norman kings and nobles hunted with passion. Their obsession found expression in every aspect of life. A finely carved tympanum, filling the space between door lintel and arch at Holy Trinity Church, Ashford-in-the-Water, incongruously to us depicts a boar and a wolf.

A carved tympanum, depicting a hunting scene, Ashford-in-the-Water.

Chasing down game with spear and arrow was recreational sport, an escape from the affairs of state, but also a way of keeping men and horses fit for battle. In mediaeval England, 'forest' did not necessarily mean woodland. It was a much broader term used to define an area where deer and wild boar – collectively the 'venison' – were reserved for the pleasure of the king and a select few of his most privileged earls. Most usually the forest was a mix of wooded coverts and open countryside. Native red and roe deer were supplemented by fallow deer, caged and imported from Europe. Before they were hunted to extinction, wild boar was treated as a kind of honorary deer.

Forest Law, codified by Henry II in 1184, was brutal. Transgressors faced blinding or the loss of a limb. In practice, fines were the more common punishment. Offenders could be taken 'Dog-draw' (with a hound chasing down a wounded animal); 'Stable-stand' (caught poised to shoot); 'Back-bearing' (carrying a kill); or 'Bloody-hand' (literally red-handed). A team of verderers, rangers, wood-reeves and keepers under the control of a steward or chief forester collected rents and upheld Forest Law. The steward presided over regular woodmote or swanimote courts. Every few years the king's own justices arrived to hold assizes known as Forest Eyre courts, pronouncing on outstanding cases and collecting receipts.

In many ways the process of declaring a legal Forest mirrored the establishment of a national park in modern times. Setting a constitutional framework, deciding boundaries and reaching – or imposing – agreements with landowners. The familiar millstone symbol marks the limits of the Peak District National Park. In the Middle Ages, fences, ditches, gates, earth banks and stone crosses were all used to inform people they were entering an area covered by Forest Law. Those living within Forest limits often retained rights of common, perhaps to pasture livestock or collect firewood, but regulations designed to preserve the vegetation or 'vert' were as strict as those protecting the animals of the chase.

History records two legal Forests in Derbyshire. There is strong evidence for a third. The 'Fforesta de Alto Pecco' or Royal Forest of the Peak covered 40 square miles bounded by the rivers Etherow, Derwent, Wye and Goyt. It was divided into three administrative wards: Campagna, Hope and Longdendale.

Campagna – 'open country' in Norman French – became anglicised as 'Champion'. Edale Cross, sometimes known as Champion Cross, the old boundary marker of Campagna Ward still stands, tucked into a recess in a stretch of drystone wall beside the footpath between Hayfield and Edale.

Ward courts were held at Wormhill and Tideswell. Those with duties in the Forest frequently held or rented land in return for carrying out their duties. Many posts were

The Edale or 'Champion' Cross.

hereditary, passed down through generations of the same family. Thomas Foljambe and the descriptively named John de Wolfhunt were granted land at Wormhill in return for clearing the Peak Forest of wolves. Wolves were hunted with traps. Even employees were not trusted in the forest with bow and arrow.

Chapel-en-le-Frith (the 'Chapel in the Forest') takes its name from the church dedicated to St Thomas Becket, built by forest officials in 1225 to save journeying to Hope, where the parish church of St Peter contains a number of memorials displaying the axes, horns and other symbols of Forest officials. The Woodroffe Arms at Hope commemorates a family who for generations held the post of wood-reeve in the High Peak.

Better known as Duffield Frith, the Royal Forest of Duffield occupied the countryside between Duffield and Wirksworth. Until 1266, the de Ferrers family had hunting rights here. When Robert de Ferrers was dispossessed for his part in Simon de Montfort's revolt against Henry III, his lands passed to the Duchy of Lancaster and became Crown property in 1399 when the Duke of Lancaster became Henry IV.

Duffield Frith was divided into four wards: Belper, Colebrook, Chevin and Hulland. The Forest Court for Chevin was probably held where Courthouse Farm now stands. St

The Woodroffe Arms, Hope.

Alkmund's Church, Duffield, contains the alabaster effigy of Sir Roger Mynors, deputy steward in the early-16th century, and an impressive monument to Anthony Bradshaw of Farley Hall, who was appointed to the post by the Earl of Shrewsbury in 1593.

Within Duffield Frith were a number of enclosed parks, some dating from the hunting revival of Tudor times. Among those whose names have survived, Mansell Park and Ravensdale Park still have stretches of the original park 'pale', a protective ditch and bank topped by a fence.

Royal Forests had their heyday in the 12th and 13th centuries. Because they encroached on the rights of landowners

The memorial to Anthony Bradshaw, St Alkmund's Church, Duffield.

The remnants of the park 'pale', Mansell Park.

they were not universally popular. Stopping their spread was one of the aims of Magna Carta, the English barons's ultimatum to King John. In 1225, a group of Derbyshire knights successfully petitioned Henry III to declare an area between the River Derwent and the River Erewash, from Spondon in the south to Chesterfield and Bolsover in the north, free of Forest Law. The name of this 'secret' Forest has been lost but the knights' action is not the only clue that a legal Forest existed in this area. Fines recorded in 12th and 13th-century pipe rolls are consistent with Forest penalties. A perambulation to confirm a Forest boundary is recorded at the time of the knights' plea.

Forest Law remained on the Statute Book until 1817. Now we are witnessing changes of a different kind. Agriculture is in decline and land ownership is as much about stewardship as farming in the traditional sense. Wild deer are notoriously difficult to count but estimates suggest there are more in England now than at any time since the last Ice Age. A small number of wild boar, farm escapees, are back in our countryside for the first time in over 600 years. Hunting with dogs has been outlawed. If he were around to be asked today, I wonder what William the Conqueror would say about the controversial hunting ban? Something along the lines of 'Tally Ho' perhaps?

16

BURROWING INTO BARROWS

The hills are alive with landscape features from our ancient past.

It is not only lonely goatherds you find high on a hill. Take a look at almost any Ordnance Survey map and you will find tumuli marked. Surviving burial mounds, the commonest of all our ancient landscape monuments, are invariably, although not exclusively, to be found in prominent places. Over 30,000 have so far been identified in Britain. Undoubtedly more remain to be discovered and the list is being added to all the time.

Most burial mounds are of the type known as round barrows or lows (from an Old English word 'hlaw' meaning mound) and date from the Bronze Age (around 2000 BC–500 BC). Barrows continued to be built or re-used in the Iron Age, through the Roman period and into Anglo-Saxon times.

When first constructed they would have been conspicuous features, shaped like an upturned bowl and surrounded by a ditch. In lowland areas the mounds are of earth, in the Peak District stone was often used. Moving large tonnages of material using primitive wooden shovels and flint hand tools would have been a tough challenge. Sophisticated organisation and hours of labour from some kind of prehistoric *Ground Force* team went into barrow construction. These monuments clearly had great significance for the people who built them.

With the spread of Anglo-Saxon culture came the custom of barrow burial for the most important individuals. Often they were buried with articles to accompany their journey to an afterlife. Recovered grave goods commonly include everyday items such as combs and drinking vessels and occasionally more valuable possessions.

In the 18th and 19th centuries, the gentry with time and money to spare acquired a passion for investigating our past. Country squires and village parsons began digging up sites with the characteristic enterprise, energy and self-belief that was at the same time painting the world map 'British Empire' pink, enabling us to plunder classical antiquity with equal disregard for the damage caused.

Modern archaeological excavation is a job for experts, a meticulous and painstaking business of sifting, measuring and recording. Inevitably, however carefully carried out, it is still an essentially destructive process. Imagine the damage caused by the early diggers as teams of men armed with spades and pickaxes carved through two or three barrows in a single day searching for coins, weapons, jewellery and other artefacts to display as trophies. The minutiae that would have added so much to our knowledge of the barrow builders smashed, scattered and thrown onto the spoil heap

There were, however, some honourable exceptions. Men such as Thomas Bateman and his associate Samuel Carrington, who explored many of the barrows of Derbyshire and the Staffordshire Moorlands, worked at speed but were also serious historians. They documented finds and their intervention pre-empted many important sites being thoughtlessly looted by less scrupulous treasure seekers.

Fortunately, barrows were some of the first sites to be protected by the Ancient Monuments Act of 1882. Our best hope now of finding more lost sites is by aerial photography. From above, the distinctive circular ditches of vanished mounds often show as crop marks or parch marks in the soil.

One of the problems with recognising and identifying barrows on the ground is the potential for confusion with other natural and manmade features. Mottes or castle mounds also tend to have encircling ditches. Mounds and cairns were erected as territorial boundary markers and burial mounds sometimes performed a dual purpose in this respect. Post windmills were rigged on high ground. Frequently their supporting timbers, known as cross-trees, were set into a protective mound that may survive after the mill itself has gone. Artificial rabbit warrens or pillow mounds were built throughout the Middle Ages. To add to the difficulty, some prehistoric earthworks have been adapted or converted, convenient readymade sites for some of these alternative uses. Small-scale quarrying, mining and clay extraction all produce spoil heaps capable of being misinterpreted.

Natural crests and hilltops were favourite sites, and barrows built on high ground had a better chance of surviving as recognisable features into modern times. Stone cairns provided a convenient source of building material and were vulnerable to being robbed out, nevertheless areas such as Stanton Moor in the Peak District remain littered with remains. On the low-lying lands of the river valleys, centuries of arable farming has ploughed out many landscape features and so barrows are less in evidence. At Yoxall, a low tumulus crowning The Rough retains its secrets. It is in the corner of a field on private land but the view from a nearby footpath makes clear the site enjoys a panoramic vista across to Cannock Chase and Castle Ring hillfort.

BURROWING INTO BARROWS

A tree-covered earthwork adjacent to Croxall's isolated church beside the River Mease is marked on maps as a motte, suggesting a castle mound. It is much more likely to be a round barrow. Barrows on lower ground are frequently associated with springs or rivers and may date from the time, around 3,000 years ago, when water cults became increasingly popular.

The site of the barrow discovered at Elford.

Toot Hill barrow, Uttoxeter.

A barrow perches prominently beside the road on farmland at Elford. It overlooks an old river crossing in the fertile valley of the River Tame below. Traces of a Bronze Age cremation were discovered buried deep in the mound in 1680. After backfilling the site the diggers planted an oak sapling as a mark of respect. The gnarled remains of this now ancient tree still top the mound. Landscape features have a way of developing their own myths over time. This particular mound has been known as Robin Hood's Shooting Butt, a reference to its possible use as a practice ground for archery.

The remaining visible barrow at Lowes Lane, Swarkestone.

BURROWING INTO BARROWS

Toot Hill barrow stands on a commanding vantage point high above the Dove Valley near Woodgate, Uttoxeter. The remains of two cremations were found here in 1860 along with Celtic and Roman pottery. There was also a conspicuous layer of charcoal suggesting that bonfires were regularly lit on top of the mound. Perhaps these were Beltane fires, lit on Mayday as part of spring fertility rites.

Students of ley lines, sometimes known as earth energy or dragon lines, have detected a ley running north-west from Toot Hill, Uttoxeter, to another Toot Hill tumulus at Croxden. The line takes in Maiden's Well, an ancient site beside Marchington Road, Uttoxeter, along the way.

Gravel extraction and building work have added precious finds to a scant collection of prehistoric remains discovered in the Trent Valley. In 1962, when Drakelow 'C' Station was under construction, the discovery of a small sixth-century earthenware bowl pinpointed Dracan Hlaw, the lost 'Dragon Mound' that gave its name to the original settlement of Drakelow. No trace of a body was found.

At least nine barrows, and possibly more, once stood in a field beside Lowes Lane at Swarkestone. As a result of erosion and farming activity only one is now clearly visible from the roadside. Excavations carried out in 1955 established a Bronze Age date with secondary interments from the Anglo-Saxon period. Subsequent work on the site has uncovered a cursus pre-dating the barrow cemetery. These long narrow avenues dating from Neolithic times are among the oldest monuments in the world. Earth banks flank those discovered at Avebury and Stonehenge in Wiltshire. At Swarkestone, traces of post-holes have been excavated showing the edges of the cursus were defined by rows of timber stakes. When the 18th-century antiquarian William Stukeley first identified cursus features he thought they might have been arenas used for chariot racing. Nowadays it is widely believed they form some sort of ritual processional way.

Together with henges, with which barrows are often associated, monuments can reveal precise geometric or astronomical alignments, forming part of a sacred landscape, tracking the seasons, the lunar cycle, and occasionally mirroring the constellations of the night sky. It is a language that draws its vocabulary from topography. The round barrows dotting our countryside stand on carefully chosen sites, interacting with the landscape to make a deliberate statement. Once that language was common currency, now we can only speculate on its significance.

17

'X' MARKS THE SPOT

Many individuals were once denied a churchyard burial.

An entry in the parish register of All Saints' Church, Lullington, dated 31 March 1644, records that Philip Greensmith was executed for desertion. He was hung from a tree at Coton-in-the-Elms. These were desperate times. The English Civil War had raged for almost two years, fortunes fluctuating with opposing Royalist and Parliamentary forces evenly matched. It was to be another year before Cromwell's New Model Army was formed and the tide began to turn conclusively in favour of Parliament.

When hostilities were first declared, in August 1642 at Nottingham, the only forces available to either side were local militias. This led supporters on both sides to raise private armies. Sir John Gell of Hopton Hall declared for Parliament and was asked by the Earl of Essex to raise a regiment to garrison Derby. Gell commissioned a number of prominent Derbyshire landowners to serve under him. They, in turn, recruited troops locally, often coercing their tenants.

Many naïve young men with little experience of life beyond their own village or the nearest market town were attracted by the prospect of adventure. Small recruiting parties marched through the countryside to the beat of a military drum – literally 'drumming up support'. The pay was good. A young man could earn far more as a foot soldier than he could expect as a farm labourer. With no single unified command structure, discipline in the militias was a constant problem. Deserters met with summary justice.

Arguably the most competent of the officers commissioned locally by Gell was Thomas Sanders, owner of a large country estate at Lullington. Sanders had been captured at Burton upon Trent in January 1644 but was freed in an exchange of prisoners and subsequently promoted to the rank of major.

On the day Philip Greensmith was executed, Sanders was in Derby. His troops were patrolling south Derbyshire on the look out for Royalist detachments returning to their base at Tutbury Castle from Ashby-de-la-Zouch. A group scouting north of the River Trent caught up with some of the king's men near Egginton. In a decisive engagement the Royalist forces were quickly beaten and many were taken prisoner. Those trying to escape were pursued, some drowning as they attempted to flee across the river using an ancient

Lad's Grave crossroads.

ford at Newton Solney. While this skirmish was taking place a second cohort of Sanders's men was in the Lullington area. It seems likely that this group apprehended the unfortunate Philip Greensmith, possibly already posted as a deserter. The hanging is said to have taken place on a tree in a field near Overfields Farm and the body buried beside the nearby crossroads. This junction, where Coton Road meets Catton Lane, is still known today as Lad's Grave.

Criminals and those who committed suicide (technically 'self-murderers') were denied the privilege of being buried on consecrated ground. Lad's Grave, a quiet rural crossroad on the parish boundary, is typical of the sites chosen to bury those individuals thought not to deserve a place in the churchyard. In around 1716, a man named Samuel Mather committed suicide at Brackenfield and was interred at the crossroads now known as Mathersgrave, a mile east of the village. His body was uncovered during road widening and reburied nearby. A stone in the garden wall of a nearby house is inscribed 'SM' with the wrong date of 1643, in memory of the event.

A crossroad burial may also have taken place on Bonsall Moor. An early 18th-century guidepost on a parish boundary near Shothouse Spring marks the junction of two old

Samuel Mather's memorial.

drovers' roads. Directions on each of the four sides read 'Ashborn', 'Bakewel', 'Chesterfeild' and 'Matlock'. Beneath is carved an additional inscription: '1757 near this place lieth…' but the name has weathered away and is no longer legible.

The earliest recorded crossroad burial dates from 1510 and concerns a Suffolk monk who hung himself after accusations of misappropriating priory funds. The custom is almost certainly older, probably dating back to soon after the re-introduction of Christianity in Anglo-Saxon times. It continued until an Act of Parliament abolished the practice for good in 1823.

Standing at the crossroads. It is a powerful symbol, a physical meeting of the ways, a potent metaphor for life-changing decisions and a sign freighted with religious overtones. In a superstitious age it is small wonder that crossroads, especially those in isolated places and on territorial boundaries, became the place for outsiders. Superstition dictated that unhappy souls unable to find rest might return as ghosts to terrify the living unless their mortal remains were dealt with appropriately. Even after crossroad burials ceased, there was an interim period when the churchyard burial of suicides and criminals took place without ceremony and at night.

Nowadays few places are remote. We travel in our cars with maps or satellite navigation systems to guide us to our destination. With mobile 'phones we are always 'in touch'. Signposts are accurate. Crossroads no longer have the meaning they held for our ancestors. But next time you approach a country junction its significance in a former age might just be worth a thought.

18

BUILDING ENGLAND

The real life story of a Henry Yeveley is more than a match for the legend of his contemporary, Dick Whittington.

Like the Dick Whittington of pantomime fame, Henry Yeveley went to London to seek his fortune. Unlike Dick, Henry did not expect the streets of the capital to be paved with gold. He was much too practical and realistic for such fantasy. He knew the streets were hardly paved at all. But if they wanted the job done, as a master stonemason he was the man for the task. When the real Dick Whittington became lord mayor of London, Henry was busy remodelling the Palace of Westminster for Richard II, the culmination of 40 years as England's architect in chief.

The tiny village of Yeaveley, five miles south of Ashbourne, accounts for the family name. Around the time Henry was born, in the 1320s, they moved permanently to Uttoxeter where Henry's father Roger Yeveley was most probably engaged to work on the spire of St Mary's Church, a major building project. For Roger Yeveley it was the start of a thriving business as a mason, he bought property in Uttoxeter and settled his family in the town.

Joining the family firm, Henry trained initially as a tomb carver. Local alabaster providing the perfect medium in which to develop his skills and create detailed monuments.

In 1348, Bubonic Plague – the Black Death – reached England. Subsequent outbreaks claimed an estimated one-third of the population. Skills and labour were suddenly in very short supply, and craftsmen doubled their prices. Henry Yeveley saw his opportunity and moved to London where he quickly gained a reputation as a mason and designer. By 1353, he was a Freeman of the City of London and shortly afterwards engaged by Edward, the Black Prince, to build Kennington Palace. Contractors for such projects had to demonstrate they possessed sufficient personal capital and resources to complete the job. Henry Yeveley's ability to accept such a commission is a clear indication of his flourishing business achievements. With Kennington Palace under his belt, Henry was appointed to work for Edward III, and went on to serve Richard II and Henry IV. Officially, his job title was 'deviser of the king's masonry', effectively he was England's chief architect.

In the years that followed, the work attributed to Yeveley includes churches (St Nicholas, Arundel), abbeys (the nave, cloisters and west porch at Westminster) and cathedrals (the nave and the Black Prince's Chantry at Canterbury; the Neville Screen at Durham). There were also great castles (Bodiam, Sussex; Cowling, Kent; Nunney, Somerset), colleges (Cobham, Kent), palaces, bridges and royal monuments. Among the memorials commissioned was a magnificent monument to Blanche of Lancaster, John of Gaunt's first wife, for which in 1368, Yeveley ordered six wagonloads of finest quality alabaster from the quarries at Fauld. The resulting, reportedly magnificent, work was destroyed when the Great Fire of London engulfed St Paul's Cathedral. Fauld alabaster was also sent to Yeveley's London workshop in 1369 to be carved into a fitting tomb for Queen Philippa, wife of Edward III. Militarily, Yeveley was involved in designing battlefield defences for the emerging tactics of combining archers and mounted knights in two-pronged assaults and in building defensive coastal towers against the ever-present threat of invasion by the French.

Henry Yeveley did not work alone. Two men in particular deserve to share the credit for his achievements: William Wynford, chief collaborator on many of the projects undertaken; and Hugh Herland, who was responsible for some fine carpentry. Herland's work for Yeveley included the magnificent hammerbeam roof of Westminster Hall, part of the contract to remodel the Palace of Westminster and one of the best surviving examples of Yeveley's genius.

At the same time as Henry was chief architect to the King, Geoffrey Chaucer also held a royal appointment as clerk of works and this is more than simply the tale of a local boy made good. It is about the making of England itself. In the same way that Chaucer's *Canterbury Tales* marks the founding of an English literary tradition, Yeveley established for the first time a distinctive and purely English form of architecture. Before 1066, this was a land of wooden buildings. The Norman Conquest brought change and new, continental ideas. Castles and monasteries were built in the austere and solid Norman French style: characterised by massive stone walls and rounded arches decorated with chevron, dogtooth and beakhead designs. For more than two centuries the kings of England were more French than English. The great monastic houses owed their allegiance to mother establishments on the other side of the English Channel. The sons of nobles were educated in France. Latin and French were the languages of administration and court.

All this began to change in the 14th century. English became the dominant language and for the first time a vernacular style of architecture appeared. Known as

The great east window, St Mary and St Barlok, Norbury.

'Perpendicular', it differed from what had gone before by its emphasis on vertical space and light. Buttresses were slimmed down and made more elegant. Perfect proportions were combined in angular, linear patterns. New techniques in timber, significantly the use of projecting hammerbeams to support the weight of the roof without the need for tie beams running the width of a building, opened up roof space. Complex vaulting, flamboyant window tracery and flattened arches with square surrounds were also introduced.

It is tempting to see the hand of a young Henry Yeveley in the conception and design of the chancel at St Mary and St Barlok at Norbury. The church sits on a scarp above the River Dove, just six miles from the Yeveley home in Uttoxeter, even closer to the family's roots in Yeaveley. It would explain why an obscure early-14th century rural parish church is, in architectural terms, an evolutionary stepping-stone; possibly the country's earliest example of a defining tradition in building styles and clearly the work of a confident, visionary designer/mason. In particular the delicate panel tracery of the great east window anticipates the emerging architectural style. Not fully realised Perpendicular but with the same sense of scale.

Did Henry Yeveley leave a legacy at Norbury before finding fame and fortune in London? Did he ever return to work in Derbyshire? We have no confirmatory records but can assume occasional visits to the area took place. Yeveley's regular use of Derbyshire alabaster would have involved dealing with local quarries, negotiating prices and selecting material. Then there was Henry's position at court. Yeveley had a close business relationship with John of Gaunt, Duke of Lancaster. Not only did he carry out architectural commissions for the Duke he also rented property to him in London. Regular dealings with the man who was virtually ruler of England must have led to invitations to visit John at home in his Duchy of Lancaster headquarters at Tutbury Castle. It is also probable that Chaucer, a frequent partner on national building projects, would occasionally have been a fellow guest. John of Gaunt's mistress and eventual third wife, Catherine Swynford, and Chaucer's wife, Philippa Roet, were sisters. The Duke of Lancaster acted as patron to the poet, giving him an annual allowance to support his writing and securing promotion for the young man early on in his career at court.

In the prologue to his *Wife of Bath* tale, Chaucer mentions the Dunmow Flitch. We may imagine Chaucer the wordsmith as an entertaining guest, drawing on a fund of stories gathered before *The Canterbury Tales* were written. Could this be how John of

Gaunt came by the amusing idea of instigating a similar custom at Wychnor? This required Philip de Somerville, Lord of the Manor of Wychnor to present half a hog (the 'flitch') at Lent to any couple able to prove before witnesses that they had been happily married for the past year and a day.

Yeveley did not invent the Perpendicular style of architecture anymore than Chaucer invented the English language. But both men were innovators who defined the basic language of a style and redefined its grammar in a way that made possible what followed. The name of Henry Yeveley may not be as well known as Geoffrey Chaucer, or even Dick Whittington for that matter, but his legacy is just as important. We do not know if he ever had a cat.

19

LOCK, STOCK AND LASH

Those found guilty of petty crime or disruptive behaviour risked harsh punishment in earlier times.

'Anti-social behaviour' is a phrase we hear a lot of in the news these days. Rowdiness and minor breaches of the peace are nothing new. A recent wheeze aimed at the problem is the Anti-Social Behaviour Order (ASBO) as the government attempts to deliver on a promise to be: 'Tough on crime, tough on the causes of crime'. 'Tough', of course, is a relative term. Evidence of a more robust response in past times can still be found.

In the tiny village of Great Gate, an innocuous looking pillar of local sandstone stands by the roadside. Iron manacles are a clue that it was originally used as a whipping post for the punishment of those found guilty of petty theft (defined as items worth less than 12 pence) and other minor misdemeanours. Whipping was seen as most appropriate for women. It was a common punishment for those found guilty of prostitution. In towns and cities women might be tied to the back of a cart and led through the streets while the whipping was administered. In rural areas there was little purpose in a parade. In any case, with entertainment scarce, the prospect of a public flogging would be sure to attract a good audience.

Any one of a number of inventive punishments might be invoked for women found guilty of disturbing the peace. The scold's bridle, a metal cage fitted over the head to clamp the victim's jaws shut, was an

The whipping post, Great Gate.

A set of stocks at Chapel-en-le-Frith.

effective way of keeping someone quiet with spin-off potential for weight loss. Then there was the humiliation of being tied to a chair known as a 'cucking stool' and put on public display. The 'ducking stool', a watery variant where offenders were dunked in the river, was popular in some areas. Naming and shaming was a key part of retribution.

As an alternative to whipping there were stocks or a stand-up version called a pillory, all good fun for spectators who could mock offenders and bombard them with rotten fruit or worse. Stocks can still be seen in many Derbyshire villages, for example at Chapel-en-le-Frith, Eyam, Sudbury and Uppertown.

All of this was a long time ago wasn't it? Well, not really. Whipping and the stocks were not technically banned until 1780 when custodial sentences were introduced as an alternative deterrent. Every parish was then required to provide a secure lock-up where offenders could be confined overnight and every county had to provide a prison. Even so, stocks and whipping posts continued to be used unofficially.

Demand for cheap labour rocketed as the British Empire expanded. Until the practice ended in 1871, penal transportation was a popular option for magistrates dealing with minor offences. Prisoners being transferred to ports were manacled hand and foot to prevent escape.

The stocks at Sudbury...

...and at Uppertown.

A set of legirons and handcuffs.

Those committed by the courts to gaol were frequently sentenced to hard labour. This might be something vaguely useful such as breaking stones but was equally likely to be totally pointless. Some inmates were consigned to a treadmill, others to the shot lift. In the shot lift, prisoners formed a square with three paces between each man and passed a 25lb shot relay fashion. Most dreaded was the crank, a sand filled engine that had to be turned a certain amount of times, with each revolution registering on an automatic counter.

We do not want to go back to those days but 'tough on crime'? You be the judge.

20

EARLY CHART SUCCESS

The first printed county maps.

Sit down with a modern Ordnance Survey map and with a little imagination the countryside comes alive: hills and valleys, rivers and streams, roads and footpaths, woodland, fields, villages and townscapes. Originally drawn by the army for military purposes, most counties had been fully mapped by the 1830s. The Ordnance Survey, formed in 1791, used a 1 inch to 1 mile scale and began to standardise conventions so that the symbols used today are instantly recognisable.

Early maps tended to be *mappae mundi* or world maps. Basing his calculations on the geography of second-century Greek mathematician Ptolemy, Christopher Columbus believed he was approaching Japan when he stumbled on the Americas. The oldest surviving English *mappa mundi* (in the British Library collection) dates from the early-11th century. Although not accurate, it does have recognisable elements. Better known is a world map of *c.*1290 at Hereford Cathedral.

Written descriptions rather than pictorial representation were used in medieval times. The boundary of Rolleston described in a charter of 1008 is typical. It begins:

First from the Dove to the hatch

From the hatch to the great thorn (Craythorne)

From the thorn to the hedge

Follow the hedge to Dodslow

From Dodslow to the street

Then to Anslow…

Not quite as snappy as a modern satellite navigation system but this system of listing landmarks worked. There was no demand for maps. In any case, the skills needed were poorly understood. Few maps were produced before the Tudor Age. One of the best was by Matthew Paris. This talented monk from St Alban's drew a map to illustrate his *Chronicles*. Produced around 1250, it shows the route from Berwick to Canterbury. Apart from one or two major bloopers – Paris has the Thames emptying into the English

Matthew
Paris map
*c.*1250.

Channel – overall his map makes sense. Counties are not marked but important ecclesiastical centres are shown.

The idea of a detailed county by county survey carried out in an orderly and consistent format emerged in the 16th century. Christopher Saxton was the man chosen for the venture. Officially it was a private enterprise financed by Thomas Seckford, a well-connected lawyer and politician, but it had backing at the very highest level. Elizabeth I took a keen interest in progress. As soon as each chart was completed a copy was sent to her chief minister, Lord Burleigh. Saxton was given an official pass authorising entry to every church tower in the land, access that gave him an excellent vantage point for surveying. Norfolk was the first county surveyed. Staffordshire was completed in 1577 and Derbyshire in 1579.

Saxton's maps, decorated with elaborate cartouches and coats of arms, are colourful and informative. Symbols give an impression of the main topographical features but there is no key. Although Saxton's notes did not survive, the accuracy of his map indicates the use of advanced triangulation techniques and he must have talked to local people in order to ensure place names were correct. We can only guess why he chose to include particular features and ignore others. Rivers and some bridges are shown but not roads. Was there concern that these might prove helpful to an invading enemy if they fell into the wrong hands? England was under constant threat of invasion at the time and the Armada was on the horizon.

Detail from Saxton's map of Derbyshire, 1579.

Saxton's map of Staffordshire (1577), engraved by Francis Scatter.

Woodland may have been indicated because of the importance of timber for the navy. Saxton may have included parks with an eye to attracting paying customers for the map from landed gentry flattered to have their importance underlined.

Of all the hotels, inns and public houses in Staffordshire why he chose to give the Bell Inn alone a name check (south of Clent and now transferred to Hereford and Worcester) is a mystery. The obvious conclusion is that the inn was a singularly useful waymarker for travellers. I prefer to think perhaps a particularly tasty game pie, a fine flagon of ale or a winsome serving wench caught his fancy while he was staying there.

Elizabeth I granted Saxton a 10-year licence preventing anyone else from copying his work. Once that expired his maps appeared in a variety of formats, some of which were for pure novelty value. Among the more inventive was a pack of playing cards featuring Saxton's 54 maps produced by William Bowes in 1590.

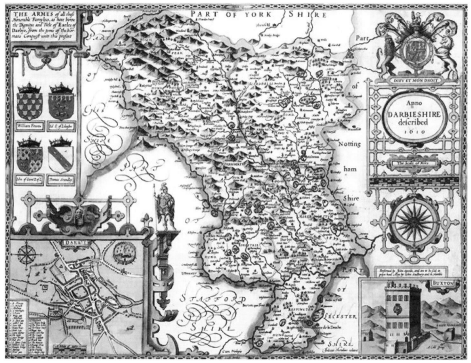

Speed's map of Derbyshire, 1610.

Partners John Norden and William Smith began an excellent series of maps based on Saxton's but with much original surveying and additional information such as distances. Unable to find a backer with sufficient capital they only managed to complete a few counties. The next important maps were by John Speed who included plans of the major towns in each county. Speed's attractive map of Derbyshire appeared in 1610.

It would be difficult to overestimate the importance of the pioneering early mapmakers. The maps of Saxton, Norden, Smith and Speed were used as templates, updated, adapted and reissued for more than 200 years.

It is claimed that while on his travels around the country, Christopher Saxton regularly wrote to his family in Yorkshire. Against my better judgement, I shall repeat the scurrilous tale that his wife struggled with his letters until someone pointed out she was trying to read them upside down.

21

DEVILISH DOINGS AT DRAKELOW

A macabre tale of retribution.

A Benedictine abbey, founded around 1002 by Wulfric Spot, dominated life in mediaeval Burton upon Trent. The monastery was not simply a centre of religion and learning, it was also a business enterprise, at the centre of an extensive and largely self-sufficient manorial estate. As lord of the manor, the abbot had wide administrative and judicial responsibilities in addition to his spiritual role. Peasant tenants (villeins) did the hard work, cultivating their own small plot in return for labouring on the manorial farm, and were legally, socially and economically tied to their landlords.

A place for everyone and everyone in their place was the basis of this interdependent social system and villeins were near the bottom of the pecking order, one up on cottagers and slaves, but with little freedom and not even able to marry without permission. According to one head of Burton Abbey, his villeins owned 'nothing but their bodies and their stomachs'. William the Conqueror decreed that peasants 'shall not leave their lands' or 'defraud their lord of the service they owe'. They were certainly not expected to think for themselves or voice an opinion. When two of the abbey's Stapenhill tenants decided to show a bit of independence and see if the grass was greener under the lordship of Roger Montgomery, on the Derbyshire side of the River Trent at Drakelow, it was bound to cause trouble.

The year was 1085. A new abbot had just been appointed at Burton Abbey. A later abbot, Geoffrey of Burton, recorded the strange happenings that followed in his *Life of St Modwen*, written around 40 years after the events described.

The abbey demanded the return of their tenants and as a bargaining counter, seized the crops of the absconders. Roger Montgomery responded by raiding the abbey barns at Stapenhill and stealing an equivalent amount of grain. Then, at the head of an armed force, Montgomery crossed the River Trent into Staffordshire. A skirmish took place with abbey retainers in open fields near a lagoon known as the Blackpool. Although outnumbered and fighting against the wishes of the abbot, the men from Burton had the best of the encounter, attributing their success to divine help.

With the seriousness of the incident escalating, the monks of Burton Abbey turned to their patron, Saint Modwen. In a remarkable ceremonial 'humiliation', an extreme measure rarely resorted to in Christendom and the only known incident of its kind in England, the reliquary containing the saint's remains was taken from her shrine and placed on the floor while the gathered brothers implored their heavenly contact to intercede. Forget any pious pleas for Christian forgiveness and understanding. The monks wanted vengeance. Ideally a bit of swift, traditional, Old Testament-style smiting. They were not disappointed. The next day, the defecting tenants were taken ill, and within hours both men were dead.

The bodies were returned to Stapenhill for burial. Late that afternoon the pair reappeared at Drakelow carrying their coffins. Occasionally shape-shifting into dogs, bears and other creatures, they haunted the village, knocking on doors and shouting for people to leave. Visitation by the walking dead continued on subsequent evenings. People became ill. Disease spread. Before long, few Drakelow villagers were left to tell the tale. A penitent Roger Montgomery humbled himself before the abbot, begging for Drakelow to be spared further suffering and promising to pay compensation.

A bizarre ritual then followed in order to lay the ghosts to rest. The villeins' bodies were exhumed and had their heads cut off and placed between their legs. Before reburial, both men's hearts were removed and placed on a bonfire. As the flames rose a loud noise was heard and what was taken by the watchers to be a possessing spirit was seen to fly out of the fire in the shape of a crow. The apparitions ended. The ordeal was over. Drakelow, with scarcely an inhabitant left alive, was abandoned. Roger Montgomery decamped to his estates in north-west England.

Brief references to 'the Devil of Drakelow', as the affair became known, appear elsewhere in abbey documents but Abbot Geoffrey's account is the only detailed source, written in two columns in neat, tiny script. Geoffrey's *Life of St Modwen* is in three parts: an introductory preface, a biography and then an account of the miracles attributed to the saint. How far can we rely on his version of the story? Did Geoffrey have a wider agenda? He certainly had a vested interest. Shrines were big business in mediaeval England and popular saints with a reputation for responding to prayer were eminently bankable, pulling in pilgrims and cash. 'Kerching' as they say today. But I think it wrong to be cynical about Abbot Geoffrey's motives. There was no mass broadcast media. Few could read and no more than a handful of copies of Abbot Geoffrey's manuscript are likely to have been produced. In an introduction, Geoffrey writes convincingly about his personal motives: 'For a long time I had felt a burning desire to find out something certain about the homeland, family, life and virtues of the most holy virgin Modwenna and I often prayed to her about this with an eager heart'.

In the abbey church, Geoffrey had the bones of a saint whose background was a mysterious black hole. It is only natural that he should be curious to fill in the blanks and bring the story up to date. Most of his accounts of divine intervention concern commonplace happenings such as accidents averted, full of detail but with no attempt at sensationalism. His witnesses are described as 'trustworthy' and their words the 'reliable report of truthful men', an indication that Geoffrey's quest, if not entirely critically objective, was concerned with accuracy. With this particular legend he was compiling his record soon enough after events for him to have interviewed people who recalled the incident. By then, St Modwen's fame was widespread and Burton Abbey already well established on the pilgrim trail. William the Conqueror himself had knelt at St Modwen's shrine. A few years before Geoffrey wrote down the results of his research, a Burtonian called Godric had been summoned to the court of Henry I to give Queen Matilda a first-hand account of how his life had been saved after praying to St Modwen.

What really happened at Drakelow? Was it a miracle as Abbot Geoffrey believed or collective hysteria? Clearly something strange and unusual took place that gripped the local imagination. Fungal diseases of grain can trigger hallucinations and offer one possible solution. Ergot, to which rye is especially vulnerable, contains lysergic acid, the active ingredient in LSD with potent mind-altering potential. Or could it have been a coincidental epidemic? Were the villeins incubating some fatal disease when they arrived at Drakelow, supplying a kernel of truth to a story that was exaggerated in the retelling? We have the evidence of today's countless urban myths to remind us how fantastic tales spread, acquiring little realistic touches that add provenance, and are soon accepted as literal truth.

22

BUILDING WAVE

More than 'just another brick in the wall'.

The humble brick has come a long way from its origins as a sun-baked mud building block in ancient Mesopotamia. Use spread around the Mediterranean in prehistory. The Roman Emperor Augustus boasted that he inherited a city of brick and left it marble.

By the time the Romans occupied Britain, bricks were recognisably bricks, longer and flatter than our modern version but similarly made of fired clay. Along with concrete, glass, plumbing and other useful building technology, the art of brickmaking was lost and neglected from post-Roman times until the Middle Ages.

By the 13th century, bricks were beginning to be widely used for newly fashionable fireplaces that were replacing simple open hearths. Brick chimneystacks were added to half-timbered hall houses to take away smoke previously left to filter through the roof thatch.

The use of brick extended during the early-Tudor age. Natural terracotta hues and decorative laying techniques added colour and interest to churches, castles and great houses, of which Hampton Court Palace was the largest and grandest.

The oldest brick building in Derbyshire is Prior Overton's Tower, now part of Repton School. John Overton commissioned the two-storey tower for his personal lodgings after being elected prior in 1437. It was one of a few priory buildings to survive acquisition by the Thacker family after the Reformation. Gilbert Thacker added a hall to the tower to create a family house. Much of the rest of the site was demolished 'for fear the birds should build there again'. Later additions now sandwich the ancient tower, incorporating it into a range of school accommodation.

Timber-framed houses began to use bricks as infill instead of wattle and daub. Laid in a herringbone pattern, the bricks produced an effect known as 'nogging'. As a basic building material, brick was slow to catch on for smaller houses. Once it did, use grew rapidly. The practical advantages were clear. Growing Tudor towns were tinderboxes of tightly packed thatch and timber. Bricks were fire resistant, relatively cheap and easy to handle. Developing techniques enabled houses to be built higher and with more spacious rooms. Better still, bricks could be conveniently made to order on the spot. If a large

Prior Overton's Tower, now part of Repton School, is the oldest building in Derbyshire.

quantity was required, beehive kilns were built for repeat firing. For small, one-off batches, simple earth clamps were made in which the clay blocks were stacked before firing to temperatures in excess of 1,000 degrees.

A 'Midland Star' style chimney, Vernon Arms, Sudbury.

The Tudors made great show of their brick chimneys, filling the skyline with great batteries of highly ornate columns. The height of the stacks helped to increase updraft. Locally, an intricate stepped design known as 'Midland Star' emerged, a distinctive regional style rare outside the East Midlands. There are excellent examples on the roof of the Vernon Arms at Sudbury.

There was no standard size of brick until modern times. Elizabethan bricks were generally smaller than those available today at around 9in x 4½in x 2in. But size, as they say, is not everything and dating bricks with any degree of accuracy requires expert analysis of their composition.

The 17th-century brick masterpeice, Sudbury Hall.

James I, accustomed to Edinburgh with its wide thoroughfares and stone built houses, was surprised to find London filled with jettied timber houses oversailing the narrow streets at bizarre angles. On arrival, he declared he would change the city's appearance 'from stykkes to brykkes', launching a wave of building in brick. Different shapes of roll-moulded, bullnosed and segmental bricks emerged that allowed imaginative designs to be realised.

In Derbyshire in the early-17th century, George Vernon turned an architectural dream into the reality of Sudbury Hall, a masterpiece of brickwork laid in attractive diamond patterns. All the bricks for Sudbury Hall were made on site, firmly rooting the grand building to the earth on which it stands. By contrast, the brick façade of 18th-century Parwich Hall looks slightly out of place beside a village of limestone cottages.

Nothing demonstrates the versatility and flexibility of bricks better than the crinkle-crankle wall. There are three that I know of in Derbyshire. Perhaps best known is the wall outside Hopton Hall. Others, less easy to find, are at Sudbury and alongside a footpath leading behind St Wilfrid's Church, Egginton. The walls at Hopton and Sudbury have both been expertly restored in recent years.

Crinkle-crankle walls, waving ribbons of brick, first made an appearance in the mid-18th century. A curving line gave strength to the structure, allowing the wall to stand without buttresses. Although eccentric in appearance they were not built purely for show. Alcoves were used for growing and ripening fruit, a process helped by circulating warm air from a stove through vents in the brickwork. Built into the centre of the Hopton wall is a summerhouse looking out over the garden behind and the fields beyond.

Crinkle-crankle wall, Hopton Hall.

It is claimed the beech-hedged Serpentine Walk, planted at Chatsworth in 1953 to frame the approach to a bronze bust of the 6th Duke of Devonshire (the 'Bachelor Duke'), was inspired by the crinkle-crankle wall at Hopton.

Crinkle-crankle wall, Sudbury.

Crinkle-crankle wall, Egginton.

Quality varies but few areas are without suitable brickmaking clays. South Derbyshire has particularly rich resources. The limestone area of the White Peak has less, but when the Friden Works began mass producing heat resistant refractory bricks for lining furnace hearths from quarries near Brassington in the 1890s they were taking advantage of clay deposits mixed with high silica sand, long exploited by enterprising locals.

Before large-scale factory production took over, brickmaking was done by hand. It was hard, demanding work governed by the seasons. Frost made clay difficult to dig. December to February was generally spent preparing and curing material dug the previous summer. Stones were removed and the mixture

The Brickmakers Arms sign.

Brickmaking scenes from W.H. Pyne's *Microcosm*.

stirred and 'puddled' before it was ready to be pressed into wooden moulds and left to slowly 'cure'.

Brickmakers gained a reputation for hard drinking and rough living but it was not only men who worked at brickyards. Women and children also laboured up to 16 hours a day. W.H. Pyne captured typical brickyard scenes in his *Microcosm* published in 1806. A number of Brickmakers Arms remain as testament to a once thriving local industry – and a desire for 'liquid refreshment' at the end of a hard day at the brickyard.

The factories, canals and railways of the Industrial Age absorbed huge quantities of bricks. Staffordshire 'Blue' engineering bricks became renowned for their toughness and durability. Staffordshire was the second largest producer of bricks (after Lancashire) in Victorian England. Brickmaking then reached a peak in the building boom of the 1960s. Since then other materials – lightweight cement-based breeze blocks and concrete for example – have reduced the need for conventional bricks. Nevertheless, bricks remain the most popular house building material.

So let's hear it for the unassuming brick. Not for nothing is it a symbol of trustworthiness and dependability.

23

IN MEMORIAM

Two related but very different memorials are on show in one of the White Peak's prettiest villages.

Ilam is one of the most picturesque corners of the Peak District, tucked into the Manifold Valley on the fringe of the National Park with Bunster Hill and Thorpe Cloud providing a dramatic backdrop. At the entrance to this compact village stands an elaborate 40ft-high Gothic memorial cross. The story of who built it and why begins over two centuries ago and is also the story of Ilam as it appears today.

Towards the end of the 18th century, England's gentry, unexpectedly and in some cases entirely out of character, began to take an interest in personal hygiene. Jesse Russell, a leading London soap manufacturer, was in the right business at the right time and – as it were – 'cleaned up'. Having made one respectable fortune, Jesse propelled himself up the rich list by making a second on the money markets with a series of shrewd stock investments. Jesse junior was the main beneficiary. An education at Eton and Oxford was followed by entrée into high society, where he met and fell in love with Mary Watts. Mary was the daughter of another wealthy businessman, David Pike Watts, head of a brewing and wine importing empire. It was Pike Watts who helped launch the career of Mary's cousin, John Constable (he of *The Hay Wain* and *Flatford Mill*) by providing financial backing for the young landscape artist in his early career.

Mary was just 18 when she and Jesse junior announced their engagement in 1809. The parental wedding present was Ilam Estate. An existing 16th-century house, formerly belonging to the Port family, was swept aside and replaced with a splendid new hall. Rebuilding did not stop there. New cottages followed for the villagers, designed in Alpine-style to match the Peakland scenery. How truly Alpine the cottages are is a matter of opinion, but in the still of the evening one can almost fancy that behind the tiny gablet windows a giant cuckoo lurks, waiting to announce the hour.

War with Napoleon's France had halted the 'Grand Tours' popular with the upper classes. Perhaps the Russells, temporarily unable to travel, thought the stylised architecture would somehow bring Switzerland closer. Mary's two brothers both died during the Napoleonic Wars, leaving Mary sole heir to the Watts family wealth when her father died in 1816, a year after victory at Waterloo had brought peace back to Europe. Jesse added 'Watts' to the family name and a magnificent memorial to his father-in-law was commissioned from Sir Francis Chantrey.

Sheffield's urban sprawl has blurred the boundary between Derbyshire and its northern neighbour. Do not let anyone tell you Sir Francis Legatt Chantrey – quite possibly the finest sculptor England has ever produced – is a Yorkshireman. He is Derbyshire through and through. Chantrey was born at Jordanthorpe in north Derbyshire on 7 April 1781. His father, Francis senior, was a jobbing carpenter and smallholder: his mother, Sarah Legatt, a joiner's daughter from Okeover, just the other side of the River Dove in Staffordshire.

After his father died in 1793, young Frank was apprenticed to a Sheffield grocer and there it might have ended. A life spent weighing tea, slicing bacon and bagging flour. An honest enough occupation but Frank was a dreamer with talent, self-belief and ambition. On his way to and from work he passed the workshop of a wood carver and art dealer called Ramsay. Here he would stop, pressing his nose up against the shop window to stare in wonder at the display. Francis had grown up with woodworking. He knew he had a gift. Putting his natural skills to creative use was what he really wanted to do with his life. At the age of 16 he managed to persuade Ramsay to take him on a seven-year apprenticeship. With his foot in the door of the art world, Francis dedicated himself to hard work. His sketches attracted the interest of other artists who visited the workshop. Among them John Raphael Smith, an established mezzotint engraver, who recognised Chantrey's raw talent and gave him drawing lessons.

Francis quickly outgrew Ramsay's and hired a room to pursue further study in his own time. He found someone to teach him oil painting techniques and was soon receiving commissions. With help from a few generous friends, Chantrey was able to buy himself out of his indenture and set up in business as a portrait painter from a rented studio in Parliament Square, Sheffield.

War with Napoleon put the great capitals of Europe temporarily out of reach, but in order to continue his studies and promote his work in an age long before mass media, Francis travelled to Edinburgh and Dublin. By the age of 21 he was dividing his time between London and Sheffield, painting portraits for the gentry of Derbyshire and Yorkshire and hiring himself out for five shillings a day as a furniture carver. Although the Royal Academy refused to take Chantrey as an official student, the authorities there were sufficiently impressed to allow him to study part-time. Francis found lodgings in Mayfair, at a house in Curzon Street where an aunt and uncle were in service. Here he met his cousin, Mary Wale.

Increasingly, Chantrey was concentrating on sculpture, and he soon had a full order book. In 1808, six of his works were exhibited at the Royal Academy, including a bust of reforming politician Sir Francis Burdett, son of the squire of Foremark Hall, with whose radical views Chantrey sympathised. A particularly fine model of another independently minded MP, John Horne Tooke, secured his reputation. Francis married his cousin Mary in 1809 and moved to a studio in Pimlico.

In 1814, with Napoleon imprisoned on Elba, the prospect of European travel opened up. Chantrey visited Paris. At the Louvre he met and befriended the great Italian sculptor, Antonio Canova. A year later, Chantrey was elected to membership of the Royal Academy. Chantrey and Canova met again in Italy in 1819, when Francis visited the master's gallery and purchased marble from the famous Carrera quarry.

Portrait sculpture made Chantrey a fortune. In 1807, a portrait in oils by Francis Chantrey would set you back around 20 guineas. Five years later, he was able to charge 150 guineas for a bust. In 1822, George IV paid 300 guineas for his likeness in marble. After that, the sky was the limit. Chantrey built his own foundry for casting bronzes. His client list reads like a *Who's Who* of the early-19th century: several members of the Royal family including George IV (sculpted astride a charger and now in Trafalgar Square) and Queen Victoria (National Portrait Gallery). William IV commissioned a statue of his mistress, the actress Dorothea Jordan with whom he had 10 children, for Buckingham Palace. There were also figures of George Washington (to be seen at the Boston State House, Massachussetts); William Pitt (Hanover Square); Sir Walter Scott; James Watt; William Wordsworth; Sir Thomas Munro (Madras); Lord Elphinstone (Bombay); Spencer Perceval (Northampton); Sir Joseph Banks (Natural History Museum); Wellington (in front of the Royal Exchange); Duke of Sutherland (Trentham Gardens) and Nelson (Windsor Castle).

Chantrey's prolific output means his work pops up all over the place in private collections, public galleries, town halls, city centres and churches. Two of his most sublime works can be found locally. In Lichfield Cathedral *The Sleeping Children* is a poignant and tender marble memorial to Ellen Jane and Marianne Robinson, granddaughters of the Dean of Lichfield. Ellen Jane died in a tragic accident in 1812 when her party frock caught fire; her sister fell ill and died just a few months later. Chantrey's sculpture shows the two girls, eyes closed as if asleep, lying in each other's arms. A model of the sculpture exhibited at the Royal Academy in 1817 touched so many hearts it was said 'All England mourned'. An innocent, almost haunting image, as if the girls might wake at any moment, Chantrey's inspiration was a 1793 memorial by fellow artist Thomas Banks of Penelope Boothby (in St Oswald's, Ashbourne).

The Chantrey Chapel was added to the ancient parish church at Ilam to house Chantrey's memorial to David Pike Watts, commissioned in 1816. Pike Watts is shown reclining on a couch reading to his family from the Bible. In this sublime work Chantrey mixes uncanny realism with classical form, feeling with restraint. Look closely and the

Chantrey's memorial to David Pike Watts.

Greek couch has Gothic moulding, something a purist like Canova would never have countenanced. Chantrey was less constrained by such pedantry.

What of Chantrey the man? Behind the hard work and fame he was considerate, unaffected and extremely personable. He made lifelong friends in all walks of life, valued those who helped him when he was in need, was quick to repay kindnesses and encouraged aspiring young artists. He never forgot or betrayed his humble origins, built a cottage at Jordanthorpe for his mother, retained his Derbyshire accent and by all accounts possessed a racy sense of humour. He is sure to have been amused by Henrietta, Lady Dillon's comment on portrait sculpture. Struggling to find a genteel way of expressing her opinion that English women had larger bosoms than their Mediterranean counterparts, she said: 'I think you'll find Frank, that Italian women can sit a little closer to the wall'.

As a guest of Thomas Coke at Holkham Hall, Norfolk, in 1834, Chantrey famously bagged a pair of woodcock with a single shot and carved the result as a present for his host's mantelpiece. He was knighted in 1835.

Chantrey died suddenly of a heart attack in 1842 and was buried back home in Derbyshire. He and Mary had no children and Chantrey's considerable fortune was left to the Royal Academy who founded the Chantrey Bequest fund in his honour. Critics may claim some of Chantrey's work is derivative but all great artists learn from the past. Chantrey's genius was to capture the essence of the people he sculpted. His natural, taut, rhythmic, fluid lines have pinpoint accuracy. Some find his memorials a little sentimental for modern tastes. Like all great artists, Chantrey is both of his time and yet timeless. We must remember his was an age of optimistic cultural romanticism exemplified by the likes of Blake and Tennyson, when the grimness of Puritan mortality was replaced by an affirmation of unique individuality and the hereafter as a place of joyful reunion.

Mary Watts Russell died in 1840, aged just 48. Within a year, a commemorative cross was erected in the centre of Ilam. Not simply a memorial it was practical too. Jesse arranged for a spring on Bunster Hill to be tapped to deliver a clean, fresh water supply to six troughs set around the base. The speed of completion was possible because Jesse Watts Russell made use of an existing design. At the time he was one of the prime movers behind a plan to erect a Martyrs' Memorial at Oxford. Leading artists had been invited to submit proposals based on the Eleanor Crosses, erected in 1290 by a grieving Edward I to mark the resting places of Eleanor of Castile when her body was returned to London from Nottinghamshire. Winner of the Oxford competition was George Gilbert Scott. John MacDuff Derick had run Scott close, and Jesse pulled Derick's design off the shelf for Mary's memorial.

Ilam Cross, the memorial to Mary Watts Russell.

One-hundred-and-sixty-five years have taken their toll. Six well-worn female figures in niches, carved separately by Sir Richard Westmacott, now protected from roosting birds by chicken wire, have suffered from exposure to the elements. Their features are eroded. Various limbs, and in two cases, heads, are missing altogether. The original buttressed pinnacle came tumbling down one stormy night. A temporary repair is still in place, incongruous but better than nothing. A verse once declared:

> Free for all these crystal waters flow,
> Her gentle eyes could weep for others' woe;
> Dried is that fount; but long may this endure,
> To be a well of comfort to the pure.

'Endure' it does, though the inscription has faded, and around the base the series of troughs, no longer needed for water, are converted as attractive flower containers.

Jesse Watts Russell died in his mid-80s in 1875. The estate was sold, the family connection severed and a formative episode in Ilam's history closed. Ilam Hall, now a Youth Hostel and field course centre, was given to the National Trust in 1934. In many ways, the whole village of Ilam is a living reminder of the Watts Russells.

Ilam village.

24

ON THE PACKHORSE TRAIL

For more than 4,000 years strings of packhorses carried goods and gossip along ancient routes.

Before the introduction of turnpikes brought much needed improvements to our roads in the 18th century, packhorses were the only viable means of transporting goods overland. They continued to serve remote rural villages into the Victorian era.

Packhorse routes avoided the main highways whose surfaces, heavily rutted by carts and wagons, often became impassable quagmires in winter. Instead they followed ancient trackways forged over centuries. This continued even after improvements brought about by the introduction of turnpikes. Packhorse-men were not prepared to pay the halfpenny or so toll for each horse and the old paths remained in use. At Bakewell, Holme Bridge offered a free alternative to the toll bridge over the River Wye in the town centre.

In mediaeval England, merchants' guilds and rich religious houses might have their own packhorses. Most teams were private hire enterprises. Thomas Pickford began one of the best-known packhorse businesses in the 17th century. Pickford's more modern transport and removal company may be a direct descendant although the link has never been proved.

Bells attached to packhorse harnesses could be heard for some distance. The arrival of a packhorse train bringing news of the outside world, gossip and occasionally personal packages from friends, was always a cause for excitement in rural areas. Salt, coal, cloth, corn, malt, pottery, lead and copper were among the products regularly packed in basketwork panniers slung either side of small sturdy ponies on a wooden-framed saddle or 'crook'. Loads of 125kg were typical. Galloway ponies and German jaegers (packhorse-men were known as 'Jaggers') were a popular choice. Occasionally mules were used. An old high moorland route from Flash crossing the River Goyt at Derbyshire Bridge was once called 'Jaggers Gate'. Estate maps, quarter session records and other old documents reveal a number of Jaggers Lanes, Ways and Bridges. A mile north-east of Nether Booth is Jaggers Clough.

Packhorse bridges are typically arched, both for strength and to allow for flooding. Parapets were low or non-existent to accommodate wide loads. Viator's Bridge across the River Dove at Milldale is an example of a packhorse bridge where the parapets are a later addition.

Holme Bridge, Bakewell.

Viators Bridge, Milldale.

From prehistoric times, standing stones in prominent places acted as waymarkers. An Act of Parliament in 1697 made the erection of guideposts by county authorities compulsory where trackways crossed. Many of these stones, known locally as 'stoops', have since disappeared. Some have been broken up or recycled as gateposts; some inscribed stones were deliberately buried during World War Two to confuse any enemy paratroopers who might happen to land.

Among the more impressive survivors are: Windyway Cross, sometimes known as 'the Long Stoop', a 3m-tall stone that replaced a much older guidepost in 1822 set on a high point amid bilberry

Windyway Cross.

Hoften's Cross.

Guidestone, Beeley Moor.

and heather scrub beside a route once used to deliver copper ore to smelting works at Whiston; Hoften's Cross, in a field beside crossroads on the A52 one mile south of Cauldon; and an inscribed guidestone on Beeley Moor, where tracks diverge to Bakewell, Chatsworth, Chesterfield and Alfreton.

Salt was among the important commodities transported by packhorse. Vast quantities were used to preserve meat. Many of the tracks trodden over the centuries became known as saltways. References to 'Salters Bridges' and 'Salters Fords' on maps provide clues to where time-worn trails crossed rivers and streams. Trackways often had a strip of paving wide enough for men and horses to travel in single file. Part of an old packhorse route leading from Birchover and Uppertown along Clough Lane to cross the River Derwent at Darley Dale has a pavement of gritstone slabs. Unshod animals such as cattle or sheep using the trails were expected to keep off the causeway.

By the end of the 19th century, the last of the packhorse trains had disappeared. Many of the old routes are now part of our network of footpaths and bridleways. For part of its length, Saltersford Lane heading eastwards from Alton now forms part of the Staffordshire Way long-distance footpath.

Saltersford Lane was once part of a route leading from the saltpans of Cheshire across the Staffordshire Moorlands to Cheadle and on into Derbyshire via Alton, Ellastone and along the Dove Valley to Ashbourne. In the Middle Ages, a

The packhorse causeway in Clough Lane, near Uppertown.

Saltersford Lane, near Alton.

A map from 1836 showing the Saltersford Lane packhorse trail and Salters Bridge, just to the right of centre.

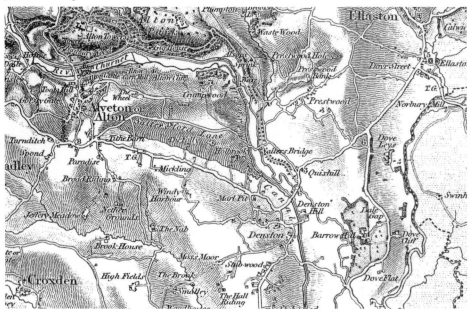

bridge replaced a ford across the River Churnet. On the first one inch to one mile Ordnance Survey map of 1836 this is still shown as Salters Bridge spanning the Churnet near Prestwood. Soon afterwards railway tracks following the contours of the Churnet Valley were laid across the ancient track. With Quixhill Bridge half-a-mile south offering a much more practical alternative for horse-drawn coaches, Salters Bridge was redundant and has vanished, leaving no visible trace.

For long stretches the old packhorse trails must look much as they did two centuries and more ago. Walking the gritstone paving of Clough Lane, or following hedge-squeezed Saltersford Lane on a quiet, misty morning, you almost expect to hear the jingling of bells and the clatter of approaching hooves in the distance.

25

WAY TO GO

Coffin roads, corpse ways and parish practices.

The idea of a parish, a collection of townships and hamlets paying tithes to support a communal priest, has its roots in Anglo-Saxon times. Parochial responsibilities grew throughout the Tudor Age, and from the beginning of the 17th century parishes began to replace the manorial system as the unit of local administration. Local life centred on the parish church and attendance was compulsory. Rural parishes in particular tended to cover a large area. In the days before mechanised transport, going to church often meant a long journey. For the privileged this might be on horseback or horse-drawn carriage (All Saints' Church, midway between Brailsford and Ednaston, still has its stable). For the majority, the travel option was restricted to 'Shanks's Pony' or 'Going by the marrow-bone stage'.

Although Chapels of Ease were sometimes established to perform Sunday services in isolated villages, only the parish church was authorised to conduct burials. Communities might invest in a wheeled bier but these were kept in the church and only used for short journeys. A few have survived and can still be seen, for example at the rear of the nave of St Chad's, Longford.

When a parishioner in an outlying area died, arrangements had to be made to deliver the deceased to the parish church by whatever practical means possible. If it could be afforded, a horse and cart was potentially the easiest and most convenient form of conveyance but that was subject to the state of local roads. Many rural byways became impassable for weeks at a time in winter. For most people even a coffin was a luxury. Bodies were wrapped in woollen shrouds (an Act for Buying in Wool, passed in 1660 to support the wool trade, made it illegal to use any other material) and loved ones were physically carried on their last journey.

Traditional routes inevitably attracted macabre epithets. 'Coffin Roads' and 'Corpse Ways' were common. A rather more delicately named 'Procession Way' leading from Coton-in-the-Elms to Lullington (where the squat spire of All Saints' Church is known locally as the 'Spud') threads between an avenue of trees whose overhanging boughs became known as the 'Devil's Arches'. A 'Corpse Way' followed by residents of Breaston,

A surviving funerary bier, St Chad's Church, Longford.

Draycott, Risley and Hopewell across the fields to St Chad's at Church Wilne involved negotiating 'Dead Man's Stile'.

A journey of several miles was not uncommon. On such extended journeys regular stops were necessary, usually places specially set aside for the purpose. On well-used routes there might be a stone plinth or wooden bench where bodies could be temporarily laid down with due reverence for the departed. Wayside Crosses, most frequently erected as guides for travellers in remote areas or to commemorate an event, also occasionally served as designated rest stops. In East Staffordshire, bearers walking from Hoar Cross to St Peter's, Yoxall, traditionally took a breather in the shade of a venerable roadside tree, known as the copt oak, whose stunted branches formed a makeshift natural cross.

Part of the 'Coffin Road' from Lea and Dethick to the parish church of All Saints' at Ashover is lined with slabs of limestone. The route follows a bridleway beneath the rocky prominence of Cocking Tor and joins Salter Lane, an old packhorse route, for the last stretch of the journey. It then crosses the River Amber by a narrow stone bridge before climbing into the village via Hollow Lane.

The 1549 prayer book, introduced after the Reformation, instructed priests to begin burial services outside the church, after 'Metyng the corpse at the church style'. Lych gates

Procession Way, Coton-in-the-Elms.

Approaching Ashover by the old Coffin Road.

(from the Old English word 'lich' for corpse) were often built at the entrance to the churchyard to provide priests waiting for the bearers to arrive with some protection from bad weather.

As the population steadily grew, parishes were subdivided and new churches were built. Breaston had a church of its own by 1719. Coton-in-the-Elms had to wait until 1846 and the Victorian boom in church building.

With increasing religious tolerance, Nonconformists made their own burial arrangements. In 1888, John Furniss of Moorhay Farm, Wigley, chose to bury his wife Elizabeth beneath a cairn of stones on the land where they had lived and farmed together rather than at the parish church of St Peter and St Paul in Old Brampton.

In an industrialised, more sophisticated, diverse and secular age, Coffin Roads were no longer needed. Routes fell out of use. Within a generation or two their once important purpose was forgotten. Just a few of the old names survive, faint echoes of our past which are still resonating today.

26

TWILIGHT OF GREEN ALTARS

The old gods are still with us.

On some subjects I can wear an anorak with the best but I am not a 'Trekkie'. However, I remember one episode of the original series in which the central conceit was that the old gods of folklore and classic mythology lived and had power as long as we mortals remembered them. If not in reality it is certainly true metaphorically. Still part of our everyday lives are the Norse gods Tyr, Woden and Thor, after whom Tuesday, Wednesday and Thursday are named, and the goddess Freyja (Friday). The Latin god Saturn gives us Saturday. In France, Mars, Roman god of war is recalled by Mardi (Tuesday) and Venus, goddess of love, is celebrated each Vendredi (Friday).

Our ancestors found their gods in nature rather than buildings. Spirits inhabited water, rocks, the earth and trees. The Celtic mother goddess Danu gives her name to waterways across Europe from the mighty Danube to our own sparkling little River Dane.

Superstitions and folk memories persist even when detached from their roots. 'Touching wood', after expressing our hopes aloud to avoid tempting fate and jinxing expectations, harks back to a time when trees were believed to harbour particularly mischievous spirits that delighted in thwarting the plans of humans and had to be appeased or bribed not to interfere. Among the most enduring of tree spirits is the Green Man, commonly associated with the oak tree. A symbol of the cycle of life: fertility, spring, harvest and rebirth, his face peering through a wreath of foliage or with leaves sprouting from his mouth, he is part of our cultural heritage.

Many a Green Man can be found staring at us from roof bosses, on capitals and adorning benches in mediaeval churches and cathedrals. A carving of a Green Man can be found at St James's Church, Longdon, near Lichfield, a building that contains another enigmatic and unusual feature. In the stonework of the south doorway, a female left hand has been incised. Cut into the palm is an inverted heart and the edge of a sleeve is shown at the wrist. Brides touch it for luck as they leave the church after marrying. A custom reminiscent of fertility rites linked with prehistoric standing stone monuments that still survive into the modern age.

Green Man, St James's Church, Longdon.

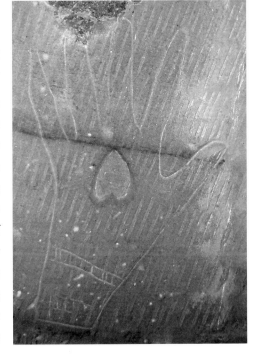

The enigmatic 'Bride's Hand' at St James's Church, Longdon.

A pagan image in a church may seem surprising but it reflects the pragmatism of the early missionaries who sought to transform and assimilate rather than obliterate the old religions. After sending back-up for Augustine's mission to convert the English – when the scale of the job became apparent – Pope Gregory wrote to his messengers in AD 601. His letter advised finding ways of adapting pagan rituals to avoid alienating the native people and re-using pagan shrines rather than destroying them. The spring festival dedicated to Eostre, Anglo-Saxon Goddess of fertility, was parlayed into Easter; Yule became Christmas. It is quite likely some pagan images were retained when sites were re-consecrated. Traditions such as churchyard yew trees, bells, candles and holy water all have pre-Christian origins.

The ancient custom of 'clypping' a church, celebrated at St Mary's, Wirksworth, each September may derive from the practice of tree worship. The parishioners form a circle around the building in symbolic embrace.

Dancing around a tree or a substitute maypole decked out with ribbons is a feature of many Mayday celebrations. The Green Man in various guises, sometimes as a woodwose or wild man of the woods, often as Jack-in-the-Green concealed under a framework of foliage, is a Mayday regular, dancing ahead of the May Queen. Are such time-honoured activities an innocent echo of the grim wicker-men rituals witnessed by Julius Caesar over 2,000 years ago during the Gallic wars when he observed: 'Great images, whose limbs, woven of wickerwork, they cram with live human victims and then place fire below…'?

Ancient preaching crosses frequently contain both Christian and pagan scenes. Saxon crosses standing outside St Mary and All Saints' Church, Checkley, and at the Church of the Holy Cross, Ilam, have carvings that may be simply abstract patterns but have been interpreted by some as depicting wicker men.

Does this Saxon cross at All Saints' Church, Checkley, depict a wicker man?

Green Man, Burton upon Trent Town Hall.

The Green Man re-emerged as a trendy architectural flourish in late-Victorian and Edwardian times, appearing on houses, banks and public buildings. A fine, stylised head decorates a door arch at the town hall in Burton upon Trent. A popular pub name, the Green Man is frequently shown on inn signs as a forester or Robin Hood figure.

It is always a Green Man, never a Green Woman, but female imagery exists in explicitly sexual Sheela-na-gig emblems. As with the Green Man, most of these bizarre images are associated with churches. Surprising not simply because of their pagan symbolism but in view of the astonishingly graphic nature of the pose, more top shelf or plain brown wrapper than page three of your daily redtop. Legs are characteristically flung wide leaving little to the imagination. Yet there is nothing erotic about these figures that are usually shown with grotesque, grimacing faces and emaciated bodies.

Sheela-na-gigs occur across Britain, in parts of France and Spain, and most notably in Ireland, a spread that clearly suggests a Celtic cultural origin. The name is Gaelic, possibly from 'Sile ina ghuib' ('old woman on her haunches'). Other derivations suggest 'woman of the castle' or 'old woman of the breasts' ('sile na gCioch'). Exactly what the image represents is a mystery. Is it a guardian spirit? A pagan goddess? A warning against lust? Or

Sheela-na-gig, St Helen's Church, Darley Dale.

a fertility symbol? Another possibility is that the figure represents mortality and the cycle of life, a symbolic return to the womb of Mother Earth. In truth, no one knows. When the Roman legions squashed the Druids, who they saw as troublesome fundamentalist insurgents with unsavoury religious practices, a strong oral tradition was severed. Britain's Iron Age tribes had no written language. Our link with the past vanished leaving mere scraps of half-remembered folklore and superstition.

There are four recognised Sheela-na-gigs in Derbyshire. I am confident of a fifth. All are connected with churches except for one at Haddon Hall. The features of the Haddon Sheela are so worn from centuries of exposure to wind and rain as to be barely recognisable. Originally it looked down from above an entrance to the stables. To protect it from further damage it has now been moved to a new position inside the stable block.

A Sheela-na-gig set centrally into a door arch inside St Helen's Church, Darley Dale, is similar in design to the carving at Haddon Hall and if anything, it is even more weathered from previously being in an exposed outside position. St Helen's occupies an ancient pagan religious site later re-consecrated for Christian worship.

Another weather-scoured Sheela-na-gig adorns the enigmatic St Margaret's Chapel building at Alderwasley.

This tiny chapel, barely 16m long by 6m wide, dates from the first half of the 16th century but it is likely that material from an earlier building was plundered for the present structure. Although villagers were allowed to worship at St Margaret's, it was a private chapel for the lords of the manor of Alderwasley.

TWILIGHT OF GREEN ALTARS

Sheela-na-gig, St Margaret's Chapel, Alderwasley.

An alabaster shield at the chapel is quartered with the arms of Lowe (a wolf passant); Fawne (a bugle with three pierced crescents); and Fogge (a horizontal band with three stars or spurs).

Alderwasley manor was in the Fawne family until 1471 when Joan Fawne married Thomas Lowe. Their son Anthony married Bridget Fogge. St Margaret's was used by the Lowe family and their successors the Hurt's until 1850, when Francis Hurt footed the bill for a much grander replacement.

Finest and most accessible of Derbyshire's Sheela-na-gigs (Haddon Hall is only open to

St Margaret's Chapel, Alderwasley.

The coat of arms, Alderwasley.

the public at certain times of the year; St Helen's Church is usually locked and St Margaret's Chapel is hidden behind locked gates); is in Melbourne's superb Norman Parish Church of St Michael and St Mary. At Haddon, Darley Dale and Alderwasley, the Sheela-na-gig carvings appear older than the buildings they now adorn. Melbourne's intricate and sharply cut Sheela probably dates from the building of this splendid church in the 12th century. If so, the master mason responsible was further removed from the age when the potency of Sheels-na-gigs was widely understood than we are from his time. Most probably it was simply an eye-catching decorative piece with no hidden meaning attached. Across Europe at this time there was a reawakening of interest in Romanesque sculpture and lurid imagery.

Melbourne's Sheela-na-gig is engraved on one of the capitals of the chancel arch. It is typically explicit with fingers tugging at private parts. Vine leaves emerge from the figure's mouth. Surrounding capitals are illustrated with equally fantastic and vividly realised scenes. One shows a grinning cat; another a dog having its tail pulled. Although not

Two Sheela-na-gigs at Melbourne.

generally recognised, what looks compellingly like a second Sheela-na-gig hovers acrobatically above a column beside the south door, holding one of the more adventurous advanced yoga positions.

Is it simply coincidence that Sheela-na-gigs tend to be found at sites linked with female Christian saints? Whatever the meaning of these indelicate pagan totems frozen in their tortured poses they certainly add to the fascination of old buildings and help to fire our imagination. And a little mystery in our collective past is perhaps no bad thing. Prehistoric spirituality was about basics. Its main aim was food, ensuring a good harvest and before the first farmers settled the land, successful hunting.

The name of the Cornovii, a local Iron Age tribe, means 'horned people'. Weathered stone carvings found at Wall, Staffordshire, show human heads with curling rams's horns and may illustrate the Cornovii dressed for religious ritual.

Cave paintings and archaeological finds of deer masks with eye slits drilled in the skull provide ample evidence of such ceremonies having taken place in prehistoric times. Abbots Bromley's famous horn dance, in which six sets of reindeer antlers and a hobby horse are taken from the village church and paraded around the streets by dancers each September, continues an event known to date from medieval times. Is it possible the tradition may descend from even older rites?

An Iron Age sculpture showing human heads with rams' horns found at Wall.

The horns in Abbots Bromley parish church and (inset) the dancers *c.*1900.

Even though the relevance and meaning encoded in our collective folk memory hovers tantalisingly beyond our grasp, blurred by the veil of time, it may still tell us something of who we are and where we came from. Connecting us to a distant time when we were closer to nature. More than that, folklore is testimony to the resilience of the old deities. It may be twilight time for the gods of green altars but it is far from oblivion.

27

SLEIGH BELLS RING

There is more to Sir Samuel Sleigh than his three marriages.

If we are remembered by posterity at all it is just as likely to be for something inconsequential or quirky than for any real achievement. King Alfred, a man of destiny and indisputable greatness, burnt the cakes didn't he? Cnut, not a bad chap as bloodthirsty pagans go, brought peace to a troubled nation but is forever remembered as the man who got his feet wet trying to turn the tide. It does not even matter if such stories are true, mention Alfred or Cnut and cakes and waves are what people recall. For Samuel Sleigh, it is the strange but true fact that more than 100 years separated the death of his first wife from the death of his third. Never mind a knighthood, serving as a justice of the peace, member of parliament, high sheriff of Derbyshire (twice) and deputy lieutenant of the county. History has always entertained a gossip column element. In Samuel Sleigh's case it was not simply the number of marriages – three or four visits to the altar was far from uncommon in an age of strict religious proprieties and high mortality. His first father-in-law also wed three times. It was marrying a 20-year-old when he was in his 70s and fathering a child that never fails to rate a mention.

Sleigh was born in 1603, trained as a lawyer and inherited the family home, Ashe Hall between Etwall and Sutton-on-the-Hill, in 1626. In 1628 Samuel married Judith Boys of Betteshanger, near Deal in Kent. Younger brother Gervase Sleigh, who lived at Radbourne, married Judith's sister Eliza to complete a family double. Samuel and Judith had just six years together before Judith died leaving two infant children. Samuel commissioned an elaborate wall monument in her memory to stand in the chancel of St Michael's Church, Sutton-on-the-Hill. The monument is an odd mix of flamboyance and Puritan bleakness. Classical columns support a decorated arch surrounded by family heraldry while a recess holds a full-sized coffin carved in black stone. Memorials to Samuel, his other wives and brother Gervase were added later. The bodies of Judith and Samuel lie close to each other in front of the altar.

Samuel married his second wife, 23-year-old Margaret Darcy of Dartford, on 17 February 1636. How did Margaret cope with being uprooted from the fringes of London and moving 'into the country' as she described Ashe Hall? She left friends and family

Sleigh Monument, St Michael's Church, Sutton-on-the-Hill.

behind, Samuel was often away on business and her sister-in-law was the sister of her husband's first wife. Reading between the lines of a surviving letter written when Margaret was visiting her family and addressed 'To the worshipful my very loving husband', suggests perhaps not unsurprisingly, that she found it difficult. How long Margaret has been away we may only speculate, but she has already received three letters from Samuel, it is clear there have been many previous visits and there is a suggestion of a prolonged absence that is the subject of criticism by her in-laws. Even so, she is clearly desperate to extend her stay and not particularly anxious to be joined by Samuel. It was probably written in 1640, a year before Sleigh was knighted. Margaret's letter is a model of dancing on eggshells. She opens 'Sir' and continues in carefully measured deferential tones:

> I acknowledg most thankfully your great
> kind-nes, and noble favour, in setting
> mee heare so often from you since you went
> into the country, I have receaved from you,
> 3, letters, being deprived of your presence,
> I esteem it a great happines to heare of
> your welfare and safety which I rejoyce in
> and pray God to continue, I desire you not
> to thinke I am discontent at your absence,
> I asure you I place my happiness in your
> contentment and in having you injoy your
> own defices, which I thinke is to be where
> you are, ordering your house and affaires;
> and I shall be loath to draw you from thence
> till it shall please you most willingly to
> absent your selfe from thence, and then I
> shall be Glad to see you the newes of my
> longer stay with my Mother and sisters, is
> most joyfull to mee I am infinitely bound
> to them for ther kind useage, and sweet Companie,
> now in your absence, my sisters presents ther
> best respects to you I beseech you to present
> my best respects to my: Brother Sleigh and his

wife I thank them for desireing my Companie I
think it pleased you to rest with me concerning
the discourse of your children I desire God
to blesse them and remember to them intreat
you my most Loving and intire affection craving
pardon for thes crude linnes, I rest *Your obedient wife*

Samuel's time was soon taken up with more pressing matters. Constitutional, economic and religious differences between king and parliament were coming to a head. In 1642, King Charles raised his standard at Nottingham. Seven years of civil conflict followed, ending with the trial and execution of the monarch.

Samuel Sleigh, initially reluctant to become involved in the Civil War, was commissioned as a captain of horse on the Parliamentarian side. Committees were set up to organise groups of counties into military 'associations'. Sleigh represented Derbyshire in a county grouping that included Nottinghamshire, Leicestershire, Rutland, Northamptonshire, Huntingdonshire, Bedfordshire and Buckinghamshire. Sitting alongside Sleigh and representing Huntingdonshire was the then relatively little known Oliver Cromwell. Sleigh served on several national committees and county commissions during the war, raising cash for the Parliamentarian cause and organising militia.

Fortunes were made and lost in a country bitterly divided. At Etwall, Sir William Gerard, impoverished by increasingly swingeing fines for refusing to renounce his Catholic faith (it was rumoured that a secret passage had been dug between the hall and St Helen's Church allowing the Gerard's access to celebrate mass secretly), had sold Etwall Hall to fellow Royalist sympathiser Sir Edward Mosley of Rolleston in 1641.

Sir Samuel Sleigh.

Victory at Naseby in 1645 put the Parliamentarian cause in the ascendancy. With the Mosley fortunes now in decline, Sleigh purchased Etwall Hall in 1646 and moved from Ashe. His acquisition coincided with the surrender of the Royalist garrison at Tutbury Castle. When orders were given for the castle to be slighted, Sleigh took the opportunity of a few cartloads of ready-dressed stone and refaced the brick-built hall with a smart ashlar façade. Margaret had little opportunity to enjoy a new home untainted by any connection to Samuel's first wife. She died, aged just 34, on 3 May 1647.

Sleigh's career continued to prosper. He was invested as sheriff of Derbyshire in 1648 and became a justice of the peace in 1650. His religious views seem to have inclined to Presbyterianism. In 1654, Sleigh was appointed to membership of a commission set up to root out and eject those 'scandalous and ignorant' ministers and school teachers who continued to use the *Book of Common Prayer* and promote High Church Anglicanism.

By the time Oliver Cromwell died, in 1658, Sleigh was becoming disillusioned with the Commonwealth, siding with other like-minded prominent individuals who were beginning to speak out in favour of the monarchy being restored subject to stricter Parliamentary control. This early constitutional rethink stood him in good stead. When the Restoration finally came in 1660 and old scores were settled, he survived, even holding on to his seat in the new 'Cavalier'-dominated Parliament.

Etwall Hall.

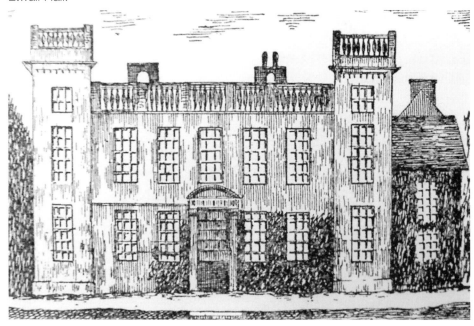

It is a tribute to the personal respect Sleigh earned that many Royalists including Sir John Coke of Melbourne Hall and Sir Henry Vernon of Sudbury Hall trusted him to handle their legal affairs. The Sleigh estate continued to grow, with land at Ashover, Dalbury Lees and Burnaston added to the manors of Ashe and Etwall.

As he wound down from public life, Sleigh chose a local girl, 20-year-old Elizabeth Harpur, daughter of Sir John and Lady Susan Harpur of Calke Abbey, as his third wife. The couple married at St Matthew's Church, Pentrich on 20 October 1677. At 74, Samuel was 13 years older than his new father-in-law. Samuel did not live to see his daughter, Mary, born the following year a few weeks after his death in 1679. Mary Sleigh married Rowland Cotton of Bellaport, Shropshire, in 1695 and continued to live at Etwall Hall. Her sister married Samuel Cheetham and moved to Dalbury Lees. Elizabeth survived Samuel by 58 years, dying in 1737, 103 years after the death of her husband's first wife Judith.

Etwall Hall, in a poor state of repair after being requisitioned as a supply centre and petrol store during World War Two, was bought by Derbyshire County Council in 1952 and demolished to make way for John Port School. If there really was a secret passage used by the Gerard's to celebrate the old rites in St Helen's Church, any traces were destroyed.

The old hall at Ashe became a farmhouse, construction of a new hall began in the 1830s. Since 1996 it has been the Tara Buddhist Centre.

Samuel Sleigh lived a full life, charting a safe and profitable course through tumultuous and unpredictable times. Possibly he was guided by the family motto advocating *Medio tutissimus*, a quote from the Roman poet Ovid's *Metamorphoses*, usually translated as 'In the middle is the safest path', a maxim finding a delightfully apposite echo at present-day Ashe Hall in the Buddhist philosophy of Madhyamaka, meaning 'The Middle Way'.

28

THE QUALITY OF MERCIA

The blood-soaked career of an extraordinary local warrior king.

I used to think the designers of Lichfield Cathedral (re-designers really, it was extensively made over by George Gilbert Scott and sculptors Robert Bridgeman and Sons between 1887–85) showed considerable cheek including Penda, seventh-century king of Mercia on the wonderful picture gallery west front. On closer inspection, I have now decided it is meant to be his son Peada, the middle letter obscured by a mixture of weathering and fallout from perching pigeons. Although one of the bit players in history, Peada was at

St Chad and Prince Peada, west front, Lichfield Cathedral.

least Christian, and his baptism into the faith was directly responsible for bringing Christianity to the Midlands. All things considered, a much more suitable figure to occupy a prominent canopied niche beside the devout St Chad than his pagan father.

If anyone is in Valhalla it is Penda. Top table too. I once wrote of him: 'He lived by the sword, died by the sword, and raised a little hell along the way'. Like the pagan Saxon gods to whom he remained faithful as the world changed around him, Penda was a harsh, brutal and uncompromising man. But he lived in violent times, and he had his good points.

When it comes to England in the period that we used to know as the 'Dark Ages' and in these revisionist times more politely call 'early-mediaeval' or 'late-antique' the documentary record is sparse. You had to do something fairly spectacular to stand any chance of being remembered at all. Record keepers tended to be monks, more interested in the search for divine meaning and promotion of the gospel than objective historical accuracy. The milestones of Penda's story come primarily from the *Anglo-Saxon Chronicle* (written by and for the West Saxons, enemies of Penda and hardly a non-partisan source), and from the Northumbrian scholar and theologian Bede, who although writing after the events he describes took place, would have known eyewitnesses.

Anglo-Saxon culture became dominant after the ending of Roman rule in Britain. A number of mini-kingdoms were established. Mercia, centred on the Trent Valley, was the last to be founded in around 585. Penda made it the most powerful.

We first hear of Penda in 628, challenging the joint kings of the powerful West Saxons, father and son Cynegils and Cwichelm. After an inconclusive daylong battle at Cirencester threatened to turn into a last-man-standing event, Penda's opponents were compelled to offer terms. The *Anglo-Saxon Chronicle* rather coyly records simply that 'they came to an arrangement'. It is likely the deal netted Penda control of Cirencester and extensive tracts of land along the Severn Valley, setting him on the path to fame and glory. Exactly when Penda was formally acknowledged as king of Mercia is not known. Some historians believe he was already ruler when he attacked the West Saxons in 628, others not until five years later. The argument for an earlier accession is that no independent, landless noble – even a member of the royal line whose ancestors ruled the Angles before their migration to Britain – would have the audacity to attack Wessex. No ordinary man perhaps.

According to legend, the Anglian kings of Mercia were crowned on Askew Hill at Repton, a vantage point with panoramic views over the Trent Valley originally known as

King Askew's Hill. It is this hill, or 'dun' in Anglo-Saxon, that has become 'ton' in the modern place-name. Repton was where the Mercian kings held court, feasting in a great wooden hall surrounded by their household and retainers.

Penda established good relations with the Christian British kings in Wales and the Marches who became his political allies. Elsewhere, he began forcibly extending his territory, pushing back the borders of Mercia. On 6 October 633, Penda defeated the richest and strongest of the Anglo-Saxon leaders, King Edwin of Northumbria, at the Battle of Heathfield. Edwin was slain and his severed head put on display. Heathfield has been variously identified with Hatfield Chase where Yorkshire meets Lincolnshire; Edwinstowe in Nottinghamshire and Bradwell in the Peak District. Hatfield/Heathfield have obvious similarities but a case can also be made for the other possible locations.

King Edwin was a Christian. His death at the hands of Penda made him a martyr. Edwinstowe in Saxon means 'Edwin's holy place' and 'Hatfield' occurs in the name of a nearby farm and grange. Close by, at St Mary's Church, Cuckney, a mass Anglo-Saxon burial was discovered in 1950. All the skeletons appeared to be male.

Grey Ditch, an impressive linear earthwork near Bradwell, dates from the right period and may have been constructed as a battle defence. Gore Lane passes nearby. The name is possibly a reference to a triangular shaped field rather than to bloodshed, but it is a name that adds something to local folklore. An ancient tree known as the 'Eden Tree' or 'Edwin's Tree' is traditionally where Edwin's remains were hung. Strange fruit and the highly-visible display of a defeated enemy leader's body sounds macabre but it had a practical purpose. There was every chance that clear proof of a leader's death would end the battle and prevent further slaughter.

The view over Repton from Askew Hill.

THE QUALITY OF MERCIA

After victory at Heathfield, Penda left his Welsh ally Cadwallon to run riot in Northumbria. A year of looting and devastation followed before Oswald, a prince of the Northumbrian dynasty, killed Cadwallon. Oswald sought revenge against Penda on 5 August 642, at the Battle at Maserfield. Again the Northumbrians were defeated and their leader killed. Maserfield has been located at Oswestry, a place-name said to derive from 'Oswald's Tree' suggesting Oswald's body, like Edwin's, was strung up for public display.

Penda dominated his neighbours. In 644, King Cenwealh of Wessex fled for his life to the court of King Anna in East Anglia. Anna was married to Penda's sister, an alliance that gave him some protection. However, deciding to abandon her and remarry was a mistake. Penda attacked, scattering the East Anglian forces. Anna escaped, returning after three years in exile spent raising an army, intent on reclaiming his kingdom. This time Penda took no chances, killing Anna, Anna's brother, and for good measure Ethelhere, the next in line to the East Anglian throne.

Oswald's brother Oswy installed himself as king of Northumbria after Oswald's death. An uneasy alliance was forged with the marriage of Penda's son, Peada, to Oswy's daughter and of Oswy's son to Penda's daughter. As part of the deal, Peada was baptised into the Christian faith and returned to Mercia with four priests who based themselves at Repton and began to spread the gospel throughout the local area.

What triggered a final showdown between Mercia and Northumbria? Perhaps continued demands for tribute backed up by the threat of force pushed Oswy too far. We can only speculate. The two armies met near Leeds on 15 November 655, beside a river known to the Anglo-Saxons as Winwaed (either the River Went or River Don). Heavy rain and flooding made conditions underfoot poor. Just before the conflict began, Penda's allies deserted, possibly bought off by Oswy in an attempt to stack the odds in his favour. Afterwards, the king of Gwynedd had to live with the nickname 'Battle Shirker'.

At Winwaed Penda's blood-soaked career came to a predictably violent end. Mediaeval chronicler Henry, Archdeacon of Huntingdon, wrote in his *Historia Anglorum* (1154):

…the earth was watered with his blood

and the ground was sprinkled with

his brains.

Within months of his father's death, Peada was murdered. For the next three years Mercia was under Northumbrian control.

According to the *Anglo-Saxon Chronicle*, Penda was around 80 years of age when he fought his last battle. Fifty is probably closer, but Henry of Huntingdon and another early writer, Roger of Wendover (*Flores Historiarum*, 1234), both suggest Penda was co-ruler of Mercia with his brother Eowa (who was killed at Maserfield) by 607. They may have had access to sources now lost. Either way he was a battle-scarred veteran. Instructive perhaps that in the Old English epic poem *Beowulf*, the hero fights on, battle after battle, challenge after challenge until, with his powers waning, he is finally defeated. What else were men like Penda and Beowulf to do? Retire? It was a heroic age and Penda was a man of his time. I suspect he would have chosen to die hard, sword in hand. The 2007 blockbuster movie of *Beowulf* played up the fantasy element of the story, reinterpreting the mix of myth and history for a digital age used to cartoon violence. Handed down from the time of Penda, the original has much more humanity and makes clear that Anglo-Saxon culture drew a distinction between toughness and mere brutality. Controlled aggression was seen as civilised and virtuous.

Penda was loyal to his allies and he led from the front. These were not days when military leaders operated from bunkers, issuing orders and pushing models around a map. Combat was fierce, bloody and hand-to-hand. Comradeship and discipline were important. In the shield wall your life depended on your neighbour and his on you. In every battle Penda was the prime target for his foes – kill Penda and victory was theirs for the taking. Many tried.

While his royal contemporaries and his children converted to Christianity, Penda remained constant to Woden (from whom he claimed descent) and the ancestral Saxon gods. Even his enemies acknowledged he was no hypocrite. Bede recorded:

> Now King Penda did not forbid the teaching
> of the Word, even in his own Mercian kingdom,
> if any wished to hear it. But he hated and
> despised those who after they had accepted the
> Christian faith, were clearly lacking in the
> works of faith. He said they were despicable
> and wretched creatures who scorned to obey
> the God in whom they believed.

Anglo-Saxon England was not all blood feuds and violence. It was culturally rich and in many ways socially tolerant. Women enjoyed an equality with men not seen again until modern times. Craftsmanship and artistry of the highest order is evident in archaeological finds such as the Anglian helmet unearthed with grave goods at Benty Grange by Derbyshire antiquarian Thomas Bateman and dated to around AD 700. On the crown was a jewelled boar with garnet eyes, echoing a line from *Beowulf*: 'The shape of boars adorned with gold glinted above their helmets'. Most famous is the Sutton Hoo treasure from Suffolk. Unearthed in 1939, the famous ship burial dates from the time of Penda and is most probably the grave of King Raedwald (uncle of King Anna). Among the fabulous armour, garnet-studded gold and Byzantine silver, a striking helmet and face mask instantly short-circuits us back to the seventh century. The prologue to *Beowulf* describes a ship burial:

> There laid they down their darling lord
> on the breast of the boat, the breaker-of-rings,
> by the mast the mighty one. Many a treasure
> fetched from far was freighted with him.

History is nothing if not an exercise in imagination. It may be fanciful, but I feel I know Penda. I doubt he would have had much truck with the kind of pomp and glitz unearthed at Sutton Hoo. Other Mercian kings certainly did but as yet no royal Mercian burial has been found. Somewhere in the Trent Valley or the Derbyshire Peaks, lost beneath some ploughed-out scatter or modern building, must lie similar glories.

Penda's courage is beyond dispute and his achievements remarkable. He rose from obscurity to become the pre-eminent figure of his age. His personal qualities of energy, strength and battle prowess built Mercia into the most powerful kingdom in the land, stretching from Wales to East Anglia and from the Thames to the Humber. Poets surely sang his deeds in the mead halls of Mercia, yet this was an accessible warlord, a man who ate and drank with his housecarles. Hero or villain? What tips the balance for me is that Penda was a Mercian. 'One of us', if you like. He may have been an awesome piece of work but he was our awesome piece of work. I reckon we'd have been mates.

Epilogue

WHAT IF?

Was there a time when a secret mission by a West Midlands man might have resulted in England abandoning Christianity in favour of Islam?

Fictional historical alternatives can be entertaining. You know the sort of thing. What if Hitler's forces had invaded these shores in 1940 when our defences were weak? What if Harold had triumphed at Hastings? Many of the dramatic events that shaped history were desperately close run affairs and the most interesting scenarios are those options that were real possibilities.

Is the suggestion that there was a time in the Middle Ages when England might have adopted Islam just too preposterous? Perhaps, but my interest was triggered during a history feature for BBC Radio Derby. A caller asked if I knew anything about an undercover mission, supposedly instigated by King John, to sound out the possibility of an alliance with the Sultan of Morocco and Spain. The deal allegedly on the table was that in return for financial and military backup, John would convert to Islam and rule England as a vassal of the Moorish state. While confessing my ignorance I had to allow that, given the circumstances John found himself in and the character of the man, the suggestion was not totally implausible.

A little research revealed the origins of this tale in the chronicles of Matthew Paris, a Benedictine monk from St Albans, whose accurate records tells us so much about 13th-century affairs. From Paris, the story was picked up and repeated by other historians, most notably William Dugdale in his *The Antiquities of Warwickshire*. According to Matthew Paris, Sir Thomas Erdington carried out the covert assignment to the court of the Moorish Sultan Murmeli, in 1208; a year that marked a spectacularly low point for King John even by the standards of his much troubled and turbulent reign.

John has had a bad press. From the tales of Robin Hood to Shakespeare's play he has been portrayed as unremittingly petty, mean and vindictive. But there was more to this complex man. He was intelligent, witty, energetic, socially accessible and capable of generosity to those he favoured despite being strapped for cash throughout his reign. How else could he have inspired enduring loyalty from so many outstanding and respected men of the age? Statesmen such as his chancellor and Archbishop of Canterbury Hubert Walter, or the forthright and brave warrior William Marshal, a man of unimpeachable reputation, probably the safest pair of hands in England at the time.

Admittedly, Sir Thomas Erdington, John's chamberlain and for a time sheriff of Shropshire, could be accused of mercenary tendencies. He paid huge amounts to the Exchequer to further his baronial ambitions and secure land for his heirs. But this was no more than what was expected and encouraged, as much a reflection of the times as of character. Sir Thomas's support for John appears to have been total through good times and bad.

But if John had a better side to his nature he was also unpredictable. A little less pride, a little less stubbornness and the worst of his troubles could have been avoided. For example, stumping up some face-saving compensation to buy off Hugh Lusignan, whose 12-year-old fiancée, Isabel of Angoulême, John whisked away and married. By petitioning King Philip of France for redress, the affronted Count provided a pretext for the hostilities that broke out after John added Brittany to his French possessions on the death, probably murder, of his nephew and rival, Arthur. In the conflict that followed John lost control not only of Brittany but also Maine, Anjou and the bitterest blow, Normandy. A French invasion of England was a serious danger.

When John's appeal to Pope Innocent III for support in his dispute with France was ignored the seeds of future confrontation were sown. Tension between the two exploded when Hubert Walter died. John's choice to take over as Archbishop of Canterbury was John Gray, Bishop of Norwich. The monks of the chapter at Canterbury decided to elect a sub-prior from their own number. Innocent III was asked to adjudicate. He responded by refusing both candidates, nominating Cardinal Stephen Langton instead. John was outraged. He had not even met Langton and rejected him outright. When Pope Innocent pressed ahead with Langton's consecration John seized Canterbury Cathedral along with its assets and banished the monks. In many ways the entire affair was a pointless power struggle, a petulant piece of posturing and interfering by all concerned. Challenged by authority the monks were always going to back down and the Pope had exceeded his authority. But the jockeying for ascendancy between two such powerful, vain and determined men raised the stakes. Neither was prepared to give ground.

A papal clerk, Pandulf, was sent to negotiate and the Pope appointed a commission of bishops to adjudicate. Faced with John's intransigence they resorted to the ultimate sanction. In March 1208, England was placed under an Interdict and the king himself excommunicated. With the Church so central to national life this was a major disruption.

Services were suspended, except for the baptism of children and hearing confession from the dying. It took a heavy-handed combination of cajolery, coercion and bribery from John in order to maintain to some semblance of normality.

Even worse for John, the Interdict was the equivalent of a Papal blessing for any invasion of England. A point not lost on Philip of France who once more threatened to attack. At home, John's personal excommunication cast doubts on the validity of the oaths of allegiance made to him by his barons.

Caught between so many rocks and hard places, might the beleaguered John have thought the unthinkable – an alliance with the Moors? In 1208, he was backed into a very tight corner and in desperate need of a strong ally. To a pragmatist with few scruples and a penchant for mischief there would have been definite attractions. As for his own beliefs although John was buried in a monk's habit he rarely attended mass as an adult. Possibly being packed off to the Loire Valley for indoctrination by the brothers at Fontevrault Abbey as an infant had the opposite effect and turned him off religion altogether. Growing up in the shadow of Richard the Lionheart, his fiercely devout and robust elder sibling, cannot have been easy. All the evidence suggests John was at best a religious sceptic. An expedient conversion to Islam would be unlikely to cause him any hang-ups or doctrinal qualms. We should also remember that in many ways this was the golden age of Islamic culture: relatively tolerant, intellectually and artistically flourishing.

If preliminary overtures to the Moorish Sultan were made, was John serious? Undoubtedly rash on occasions, John was not stupid. It is unlikely he would risk adding to a growing list of powerful enemies by involving the Sultan in nothing more than an elaborate bluff. Also, if the mission was intended as a pressure ploy in the negotiations with the Pope, why keep it a secret at the time?

Could John have delivered his side of the bargain if the offer had been accepted? There is a clue to the mood of the country in the eventual reconciliation with Rome. After five years under the Interdict, John swallowed his pride and agreed a deal with the Pope. In many ways the pact was remarkably similar to his supposed offer to the Sultan, Murmeli. John swore to uphold the faith and accept the Pope as England's overlord. The country was divided. Some backed the decision and others felt England was being sold out.

It was a remarkable turnaround. With Pope Innocent's blessing, John now took the vows of a crusader and raised an army to deal with his opponents. The forces ranged against him were augmented by a large French contingent led by the Dauphin, Louis. Months of civil war followed.

If any alliance between John and Murmeli had been formed, civil war on some scale was the most likely outcome. Would this have spread to engulf Europe? Or would a finely poised power balance have maintained a precarious peace? Would the country at large have embraced Islam? From our 21st-century perspective we can only guess at the extent of any backlash of feeling against a high-handed Church and what the longer-term implications might have been.

INDEX